Navigating the Right to Housing

Studies in Housing Law Volume 5

A series of peer-reviewed papers on the topic of housing law broadly conceived including doctrinal, jurisprudential, theoretical and socio-legal contributions from scholars of housing law based globally.

Published by Eleven, The Hague, the Netherlands

Navigating the Right to Housing

Exploring the Complex Landscape of Access, Occupancy, and Exit Rights

Michelle Bruijn and Stefan van Tongeren (Eds.)

eleven

Published, sold and distributed by Eleven
P.O. Box 85576
2508 CG The Hague
The Netherlands
Tel.: +31 70 33 070 33
Fax: +31 70 33 070 30
e-mail: sales@elevenpub.nl
www.elevenpub.com

Sold and distributed in USA and Canada
Independent Publishers Group
814 N. Franklin Street
Chicago, IL 60610, USA
Order Placement: +1 800 888 4741
Fax: +1 312 337 5985
orders@ipgbook.com
www.ipgbook.com

Eleven is an imprint of Boom (Den Haag).

ISBN 978-90-4730-221-6
ISBN 978-94-0011-419-7 (E-book)

The research presented in this book has received funding from the European Union's erc Research Grant under grant agreement No 949316.

Funded by the European Union

European Research Council
Established by the European Commission

Preface

Navigating the Right to Housing is the fifth volume in a series that aims to explore the various aspects of housing law from different academic and professional perspectives. Edited by Michelle Bruijn and Stefan van Tongeren, it is divided into three parts and contains twenty-four papers covering the entire spectrum of the right to housing.

The book is a compilation of papers written by research assistants, Ph.D. students, and senior researchers working on **the EVICT project**, a European Research Council (ERC) Starting Grant project (grant agreement No 949316). The EVICT project is a collaboration between legal scholars and computational linguists and combines legal research with data science techniques to investigate whether and how the international right to housing prevents people from being evicted.

The research assistants who contributed to this volume are Maria Anghel, Andrei-Fabian Balan, Emma Bowar, Matleena Gurara, Sarah Manohar, Phoebe Muir, Maria Niemelä, Gabriel Osinga, Lea Schubert, and Kati Vainionpää. Further contributions have been made by Ph.D. students Els Schipaanboord, Emma Sweeney, and Roos Wind. The general introduction on the conceptualisation of the right to housing has been written by the Principal Investigator of the EVICT project, Michel Vols. The introductions to the three parts of this volume – Access Rights, Occupancy Rights and Exit Rights – have been written by Michelle Bruijn and Stefan van Tongeren, editors of this volume and researchers working on the EVICT project.

Michelle Bruijn and Stefan van Tongeren
Groningen, March 6th, 2024

Table of Contents

Conceptualising the Right to Housing

Michel Vols

1 Introduction

This edited volume is a valuable addition to the existing knowledge on the right to adequate housing. The papers in this volume provide detailed descriptions of contemporary housing issues and case law related to the right to adequate housing. The authors' focus on countries often overlooked in the field of housing law scholarship is commendable. Moreover, the volume enriches our conceptual understanding of the right to adequate housing by expanding on the typology of access rights, occupancy rights, and exit rights to housing.

Several studies have described the right to adequate housing in particular treaties or countries. Even so, these descriptions often offer a limited understanding of the right's more conceptual and abstract meaning. While they help interpret the right to adequate housing in a specific national or treaty context, they do not provide a deeper insight into the overall understanding of the right to housing.

Some publications focus on the more abstract meaning of the right to housing.[1] Fitzpatrick and others, for example, distinguish between the right to adequate housing and housing rights. The former is for those who lack minimally adequate accommodation, while the latter refers to protection from eviction and harassment for those who already have housing. According to the authors, there are legal rights to housing that can be enforced by individuals in domestic courts. Additionally, a programmatic approach binds the state and public authorities to develop and implement social policies.[2]

1 See, among others, B. Bengtsson, 'Housing as a Social Right: Implications for Welfare State Theory', Scandinavian Political Studies, Vol. 24, No. 4, 2001, pp. 255-275; C.U. Schmid, 'The Right to Housing as a Right to Adequate Housing Options: Reviewing the Reasonableness of National Housing Policies in the Field of Alternative and Intermediate Tenures', European Property Law Journal, Vol. 9, No. 2-3, 2020, pp. 157-178.

2 S. Fitzpatrick, B. Bengtsson & B. Watts, 'Rights to Housing: Reviewing the Terrain and Exploring a Way Forward', Housing, Theory and Society, Vol. 31, No. 4, 2014, p. 453.

Hohmann also makes a distinction between the right to housing and housing rights. The former refers to a human right codified or implied in international and regional rights covenants and domestic constitutional orders. On the other hand, housing rights arise from non-constitutional domestic laws of states and may include tenancy regulations and social housing provisions.[3] Hohmann argues that the right to housing is essential for fulfilling other needs and goods and may be protected by other rights such as privacy, freedom of expression, and property.[4]

In an abstract sense, the right to adequate housing could also be conceptualised as multiple interconnected housing rights, which can be classified into three types: access, occupancy, and exit rights.[5] Traces of these *rights to housing* can be found in various articles in various treaties and constitutions. I will discuss this conceptualisation in more detail in the remainder of this paper.

2 Access to Housing Rights

Access rights refer to an individual's right to enter or obtain (affordable) housing through ownership, rental, or other means. They are relevant when people want to enter, acquire, rent, or in any other way start using housing. The main concerns are obstacles to the enjoyment of access rights, which are (physical) barriers that prevent individuals from utilising housing and the lack of available, affordable, and adequate housing. Various human rights documents contain references to access rights. For example, Article 19 of the (non-binding) European Pillar of Social Rights stipulates that access to social housing or good-quality housing assistance needs to be provided for those in need.[6] Another example is Article 31 of the Revised European Social Charter. This provision requires state parties to undertake measures designed to promote access to housing of an adequate standard and to make the price of housing accessible to those without sufficient resources.[7]

---

3 J.M. Hohmann, 'Housing as a Right', in K. Young & M. Langford (Eds.), Oxford Handbook on Economic, Social and Cultural Rights, Oxford, Oxford University Press, 2022, para. 2.

4 J.M. Hohmann, 'Property and the Right to Housing: Synergies and Tensions', in N. Graham, M. Davies & L. Godden (Eds.), The Routledge Handbook of Property, Law and Society, London, Routledge, 2022, p. 128.

5 See M. Vols, 'Het Recht Op Huisvesting En de Nederlandse Grondwet: Een Analyse van Artikel 22 Lid 2 Grondwet: Het Recht Op Voldoende Woongelegenheid', NJCM Bulletin. Nederlands Tijdschrift Voor de Mensenrechten, Vol. 47, No. 2, 2022, pp. 147-167.

6 See S. Garben, 'The European Pillar of Social Rights: An Assessment of Its Meaning and Significance', Cambridge Yearbook of European Legal Studies, Vol. 21, 2019, pp. 101-127.

7 E. Sweeney, L.M. Bruijn & M. Vols, 'Deconstructing the Eviction Protections under the Revised European Social Charter: A Systematic Content Analysis of the Interplay between the Right to Housing and the Right to Property', Human Rights Law Review, Vol. 23, No. 4, 2023, pp. 1-25.

In some cases, physical obstacles can hinder certain individuals from being able to live in a house. The inability to enter or move around a property freely can be a major obstacle to accessing suitable housing. These barriers may stem from the building's layout or the surrounding area. Articles 9 and 19 of the Convention on the Rights of Persons with Disabilities are highly relevant in this context.[8]

Individuals can face other obstacles when trying to access housing, some of which may be caused by others. While some of these human obstacles may be justifiable, such as a resident blocking other residents from entering their homes without permission, others may not be.[9] For instance, landlords may refuse to lease a property to tenants because of their gender, sexual orientation, religious beliefs, or criminal background.[10] This form of discrimination violates human rights law and has been extensively studied in housing literature.[11]

Of course, discrimination in the housing system can be systemic, too.[12] These and other systemic obstacles may hinder access to housing significantly. Systemic obstacles in the housing system relate to property rights and registration, housing finance, residential infrastructure, regulation, and housing subsidies.[13] A market-based approach to housing can exclude those who cannot afford it. Governments may intervene and provide free or affordable housing to the population to address market failures and excesses. A considerable number of national constitutions oblige governments to do so. This challenges the free market approach, where the state is only responsible for ensuring property and contract law rights.[14]

8 O. Lewis & G. Richardson, 'The Right to Live Independently and Be Included in the Community', International Journal of Law and Psychiatry, Vol. 69, 2020.

9 See, for example, ECtHR 14 March 2017, no. 66610/10 (Yevgeniy Zakharov v. Russia); ECtHR 8 September 2022, no. 1434/14 (Jansons v. Latvia).

10 See, for example, J.H.S van Tongeren, 'Housing Ex-Offenders in the Netherlands: Balancing Neighbourhood Safety and Human Rights', European Journal on Criminal Policy and Research, Vol. 28, No. 1, 2022, pp. 57-77; I.R. Aliu, 'Gender, Ethnicity and Residential Discrimination: Interpreting Implicit Discriminations in Lagos Rental Housing Market', Journal of Housing and the Built Environment, Vol. 39, 2024, pp. 77-102.

11 J.C Benito Sanchez, Applying International and European Anti-Discrimination Law to the Housing Context, 2nd ed., London, Bloomsbury Publishing, 2023.

12 A.M. Dickerson, 'Systemic Racism and Housing', Emory Law Journal, Vol. 70, 2020, p. 1535; P. Wolifson, S. Maalsen & D. Rogers, 'Intersectionalizing Housing Discrimination under Rentier Capitalism in an Asset-Based Society', Housing, Theory and Society, Vol. 40, No. 3, 2023, pp. 335-355.

13 P. Kenna, 'Can Housing Rights Be Applied to Modern Housing Systems?', International Journal of Law in the Built Environment, Vol. 2, No. 2, 2010, p. 108.

14 Ibid.

3 Occupancy Rights

Occupancy rights apply when residents face limitations in enjoying their residence, such as unauthorised entries. Many constitutions lay down the inviolability of the home and protect people against home searches. This protection is also offered by, for example, Article 17 of the International Covenant on Civil and Political Rights (ICCPR) and Article 16 of the Convention on the Rights of the Child.

Occupancy rights are closely linked to classical notions of privacy and domesticity, including the freedom to do as one pleases within the confines of one's home. Walzer describes this idea eloquently:

> 'Our homes are our castles' was first of all the claim of people whose castles were their homes, and it was for a very long time an effective claim only for them. Now its denial is an occasion for indignation and outrage even among ordinary citizens. We greatly value our privacy, whether or not we do odd and exciting things in private.[15]

Occupancy rights protect individuals from paternalistic or moralistic restrictions on their behaviour within their homes. Individuals should be free to read books they like, decorate their homes, and eat and drink as (much as) they please.[16] For instance, one may argue that an obligation to wear specific clothing inside one's home, such as a veil, infringes on occupancy rights, codified in, for example, Article 17 of the ICCPR.[17] The same applies to a governmental ban on drag performances that may apply to one's home.[18] Similarly, prohibiting the entry of visitors into one's home may also be seen as a violation of occupancy rights.[19]

It is also important to consider occupancy rights in cases of substandard housing or health hazards in the housing surroundings. The UN Committee on Economic, Social and Cultural Rights (CESCR) defines habitability as a key aspect of the right to

---

15 M. Walzer, 'Liberalism and the Art of Separation', Political Theory, Vol. 12, No. 3, 1984, p. 317.

16 This freedom should be limited to activities that do not cause harm to others. The fundamental debate about what qualifies as harm is beyond the scope of this contribution. See about this debate: B. Harcourt, 'The Collapse of the Harm Principle', Journal of Criminal Law and Criminology, Vol. 90, 1999, p. 109.

17 Cf. Human Right Committee 29 March 2000, General Comment No. 28 Art. 3 (The equality of rights between men and women), HRI/GEN/1/Rev.9 (Vol. I), para. 13.

18 Cf. B.V. Ries, 'Don't Be a Drag: How Drag Bans Can Violate the First Amendment', Tulane Journal of Law & Sexuality, Vol. 33, 2023, pp. 1-38.

19 H. Verbeek et al., 'Allowing Visitors Back in the Nursing Home During the COVID-19 Crisis: A Dutch National Study into First Experiences and Impact on Well-Being', Journal of the American Medical Directors Association, Vol. 21, No. 7, 2020, pp. 900-904.

adequate housing in their General Comment No. 4. This means that housing should provide residents with enough space and protect them from cold, dampness, heat, rain, wind, or other threats to health, structural hazards, and disease vectors.[20] However, research indicates that this is not always the case. In her study of building inspections in Chicago, Bartram found that many residents live in substandard housing, and Black and Latinx people are disproportionately affected.[21] In Europe, substandard housing has also been researched.[22] Data from Eurostat indicates that in 2021, almost 15% of the European Union's population lived in homes with structural issues, such as damp walls, floors, or foundations, as well as rotten window frames or floors.[23] Research has found substandard housing is a common problem in other countries such as Brazil, China, and Russia as well.[24]

Occupancy rights also entail the right to be connected to essential services, such as drinking water and energy for cooking, heating, lighting, and the internet.[25] In the Social and Economic Rights Fulfilment (SERF) Index, which measures the realisation of human rights, access to water and sanitation are two of the three indicators of the realisation of the right to housing.[26]

The other indicator of the realisation of the right to housing in the SERF Index concerns housing affordability. This relates to occupancy and access rights, as access to affordable housing is a prerequisite for enjoying it. According to the CESCR, housing costs should not compromise the ability to satisfy other basic needs.[27] Research concerning housing affordability has focused on the financialisation of housing, housing subsidies, or energy poverty in the context of housing.[28] Others have focused on the effectiveness of

---

20 UN Committee on Economic, Social and Cultural Rights (CESCR), General Comment No. 4: The Right to Adequate Housing (Art. 11 (1) of the Covenant), 13 December 1991, E/1992/23, p. 3.

21 R. Bartram, Stacked Decks: Building Inspectors and the Reproduction of Urban Inequality, Chicago, University of Chicago Press, 2022.

22 See, for example, M. Vols & A. Belloir, 'Tackling Rogue Landlords and Substandard Housing: Local Authorities' Legal Instruments and Their Effectiveness', Journal of Property, Planning and Environmental Law, Vol. 11, No. 1, 2019, pp. 2-19.

23 Eurostat 'Total population living in a dwelling with a leaking roof, damp walls, floors or foundation, or rot in window frames or floor' EU-SILC survey, 2023.

24 See M. Vols et al., 'The Right to Adequate Housing & BRICS: An Exploratory Comparative Analysis of Brazil, China and Russia', European Journal of Comparative Law and Governance, Vol. 11, No. 1, 2023, pp. 1-41.

25 For the relation between the right to housing and the right to energy, see: M. Hesselman, 'Right to Energy', in C. Binder, M. Nowak, J. Hofbauer & P. Janig (Eds.), Elgar Encyclopedia of Human Rights, Cheltenham, Edward Elgar Publishing, 2022, pp. 62-69.

26 See https://serfindex.uconn.edu/ (last accessed 15 December 2023).

27 UN Committee on Economic, Social and Cultural Rights (CESCR), General Comment No. 4: The Right to Adequate Housing (Art. 11 (1) of the Covenant), 13 December 1991, E/1992/23, p. 3.

28 See, for example, J. Hohmann, 'Toward a Right to Housing for Australia: Reframing Affordability Debates through Article 11(1) of the International Covenant on Economic, Social and Cultural Rights', Australian

rent control. Kholodilin, for example, conducted a comprehensive literature review and found that rent controls effectively reduce housing rents or slow their growth. However, they may also have negative effects that impact landlords and tenants.[29]

4 EXIT RIGHTS

Exit rights to housing refer to the rights of individuals when they have to leave their homes either voluntarily or involuntarily. The terminology used to describe these rights depends on the circumstances under which people are forced to leave their homes. For example, in situations of conflict and war, researchers may use terms such as displacement or domicide to describe the loss of homes or land.[30] The term eviction is more commonly used in the context of the right to adequate housing, often accompanied by the adjective 'forced'.[31] Many studies on the right to adequate housing have focused on the protection UN treaties such as the ICESCR provide against such (forced) evictions.[32]

Research focusing on countries or regions shows that evictions occur on all continents.[33] Most of the research on evictions in Africa focuses on the situation in South Africa. It assesses how the right to housing, as laid down in Article 26 of the South African

Journal of Human Rights, Vol. 26, No. 2, 2020, pp. 292-307; Hesselman, 2022, pp. 62-69; T. Slater, Shaking Up the City: Ignorance, Inequality, and the Urban Question, Berkley, University of California Press, 2021, pp. 84-108.

29 K.A. Kholodilin, Rent Control Effects through the Lens of Empirical Research: An Almost Complete Review of the Literature, Berlin, Deutsches Institut für Wirtschaftsforschung, 2022.

30 See, for example, M. Morel, The Right Not to Be Displaced in International Law, Cambridge, Intersentia, 2014; B. Akesson & A.R. Basso, From Bureaucracy to Bullets: Extreme Domicide and the Right to Home, New Brunswick, Rutgers University Press, 2022.

31 For the conceptual difference between eviction and forced eviction, see: M. Vols & E.D. Kusumawati, 'The International Right to Housing, Evictions and the Obligation to Provide Alternative Accommodation: A Comparison of Indonesia and the Netherlands', Asia-Pacific Journal on Human Rights and the Law, Vol. 21, No. 2, 2020, pp. 239-241.

32 S. Wilson, 'The Right To Adequate Housing', in J. Dugard, B. Porter, D. Ikawa & L. Chenwi (Eds.), Research Handbook on Economic, Social and Cultural Rights as Human Rights, Cheltenham, Edward Elgar Publishing, 2020, pp. 180-201; S. Liebenberg, 'Between Sovereignty and Accountability: The Emerging Jurisprudence of the United Nations Committee on Economic, Social and Cultural Rights Under the Optional Protocol', Human Rights Quarterly, Vol. 42, No. 1, 2020, pp. 48-84; N.H. Grohmann, 'Tracing the Development of the Proportionality Analysis in Relation to Forced Evictions under the ICESCR', Human Rights Law Review, Vol. 22, No. 3, 2022, pp. 1-24; M. Vols, 'The Optional Protocol to the ICESCR, Homelessness and Moral Hazard: The Alternative Adequate Housing Requirement in the CESCR's Jurisprudence – an Incentive Not to Pay for Housing?', International Human Rights Law Review, Vol. 12, No. 1, 2023, pp. 1-25; K. Casla, 'The Right to Property Taking Economic, Social, and Cultural Rights Seriously', Human Rights Quarterly, Vol. 45, No. 2, 2023, pp. 171-204.

33 M. Vols et al., 'Common Trends in Eviction Research: A Systematic Literature Review', in M. Vols & C. Schmid (Eds.), Houses, Homes and the Law, The Hague, Eleven International Publishing, 2019, pp. 1-88.

Constitution, helps residents stay put in their homes.[34] Evictions and the right to housing have also been studied in Australia.[35] In Europe, publications have focused on the protection offered by Article 8 of the European Convention on Human Rights (ECHR), European Union Law or the Revised European Social Charter.[36] Studies on evictions and the right to housing in Asia and South America are less available in English, but this does not mean evictions are less common there.[37] After the publication of Desmond's *Evicted* in 2016, a surge of literature on evictions has been published in North America.[38] Most of the American studies do not consider how eviction practices relate to the right to adequate housing, as the United States did not ratify treaties such as the ICESCR or the Convention on the Rights of the Child (CRC), nor did it codify a right to housing in its constitution. However, the government and researchers in Canada seem more open to international human rights law and comparative analysis.[39]

34 G. Muller & S. Viljoen, Property in Housing, Cape Town, Juta, 2021; M. Wilhelm-Solomon, The Blinded City: Ten Years in Inner-City Johannesburg, London, Picador, 2022.

35 J. Hohmann, 'A Right to Housing for the Victorian Charter of Human Rights and Responsibilities? Assessing Potential Models under the International Covenant on Economic, Social and Cultural Rights; the European Social Charter; and the South African Constitution', Monash University Law Review, Vol. 48, No. 2, 2022, pp. 132-159; B. Swannie, 'Protection from Forced Eviction: What Rights Do Social Housing Tenants Have under Human Rights Charters?', Australian Journal of Human Rights, Vol. 29, No. 1, 2023, pp. 23-43.

36 S. Nield & E. Laurie, 'The Private-Public Divide and Horizontality in the English Rental Sector', Public Law, Vol. 64, No. 4, 2019, pp. 724-745; P. Kenna & H. Simón-Moreno, 'Towards a Common Standard of Protection of the Right to Housing in Europe through the Charter of Fundamental Rights', European Law Journal, Vol. 25, No. 6, 2019, pp. 608-622; M. Vols, 'European Law and Private Evictions: Property, Proportionality and Vulnerable People', European Review of Private Law, Vol. 27, No. 4, 2019, pp. 719-752; S. Fick & M. Vols, 'Horizontality and Housing Rights Protection against Private Evictions from a European and South African Perspective', European Journal of Comparative Law and Governance, Vol. 9, No. 2, 2022, pp. 118-151; K. Casla, 'Unpredictable and Damaging? A Human Rights Case for the Proportionality Assessment of Evictions in the Private Rental Sector', European Human Rights Law Review, Vol. 2022, No. 3, 2022, pp. 253-272; Sweeney et al., 2023.

37 See, for example, A. Mukherjee, The Legal Right to Housing in India, Cambridge, Cambridge University Press, 2019; M. Vols & E.D. Kusumawati, 'The International Right to Housing, Evictions and the Obligation to Provide Alternative Accommodation: A Comparison of Indonesia and the Netherlands', Asia-Pacific Journal on Human Rights and the Law, Vol. 21, No. 2, 2020, pp. 237-269.

38 M. Desmond, Evicted: Poverty and Profit in the American City: Matthew Desmond, 1st ed., London, Penguin Books, 2017; E. Sullivan, Manufactured Insecurity: Mobile Home Parks and Americans' Tenuous Right to Place, 1st ed., Berkley, University of California Press, 2018; E.A. Benfer et al., 'COVID-19 Housing Policy: State and Federal Eviction Moratoria and Supportive Measures in the United States during the Pandemic', Housing Policy Debate, Vol. 33, No. 6, 2023, pp. 1390-1414; Slater, 2021.

39 M. Gallié, Eviction and International Obligations: Security of Tenure in Canada, Ottawa, Canadian Human Rights Commission, 2023.

5 HOMELESSNESS AND THE TYPOLOGY OF ACCESS, OCCUPANCY, AND EXIT RIGHTS

The issue of homelessness is a critical matter when it comes to the right to adequate housing. The topic of whether or not homeless individuals have a 'legalistic' right to housing has been discussed in literature.[40] However, it is important to consider how to apply the typology of access, occupancy, and exit rights in the context of homelessness.

It is evident that homeless individuals face a clear violation of their access rights. The lack of affordable housing makes it difficult for many of them to find a place to live, while being discriminated against due to their homeless condition makes their situation even worse.[41] Moreover, access rights can also be breached when individuals are forced to live on the streets. Hostile or defensive architecture, such as anti-homeless spikes, may prevent homeless individuals from making their homes for the night and sleeping on porches or benches.[42]

When it comes to homelessness, occupancy rights take on a different role than they do for those who reside in traditional houses with four walls and a roof. If we acknowledge the streets, parks, benches, flyovers, tents, and encampments as the homes of homeless individuals (which we should), it becomes clear that their freedom to act as they please within the boundaries of their homes is often impeded.[43] The criminalisation of homelessness involves prohibiting sleeping in public or begging and clearly limits the occupancy rights of those who are homeless.[44] Besides that, many of these temporary homes do not comply with adequacy standards stemming from the right to adequate

40 S. Fitzpatrick & B. Watts, 'The "Right to Housing" for Homeless People', in E. O'Sullivan, V. Busch-Geertsema, D. Quilgars & N. Pleace (Eds.), Homelessness Research in Europe, Brussels, FEANTSA, 2010, pp. 115-117; B. Watts, 'Homelessness, Empowerment and Self-reliance in Scotland and Ireland: The Impact of Legal Rights to Housing for Homeless People', Journal of Social Policy, Vol. 43, No. 4, 2014, pp. 793-810; A. Clarke, B. Watts & C. Parsell, 'Conditionality in the Context of Housing-led Homelessness Policy: Comparing Australia's Housing First Agenda to Scotland's "Rights-based" Approach', Australian Journal of Social Issues, Vol. 55, No. 1, 2020, pp. 88-100.

41 S.L. Stadler & D. Collins, 'Assessing Housing First Programs from a Right to Housing Perspective', Housing Studies, Vol. 38, No. 9, 2023, pp. 1719-1739.

42 J. Lenhard, L. Coulomb & A. Miranda-Nieto, 'Home Making without a Home: Dwelling Practices and Routines among People Experiencing Homelessness', Housing Studies, Vol. 37, No. 2, 2022, pp. 183-188; J. Petty, 'The London Spikes Controversy: Homelessness, Urban Securitisation and the Question of "Hostile Architecture"', International Journal for Crime, Justice and Social Democracy, Vol. 5, No. 1, 2016, pp. 67-81.

43 S. Ferencz et al., 'Are Tents a "Home"? Extending Section 8 Privacy Rights for the Precariously Housed', McGill Law Journal, Vol. 67, No. 4, 2021, pp. 369-406.

44 S. Ganty, 'The Double-Edged ECtHR Lăcătuş Judgment on Criminalisation of Begging: Da Mihi Elimo Sinam Propter Amorem Dei', European Convention on Human Rights Law Review, Vol. 3, No. 3, 2021, pp. 393-420.

housing. Depending on the definition of homelessness, one could also argue that individuals living in inadequate housing should be seen as homeless.[45]

Exit rights play a crucial role in the issue of homelessness. Evictions are often the main cause of homelessness, but even living on the streets involves constantly facing the threat of eviction.[46] The Homeless Bill of Rights developed by the European Federation of National Organisations Working with the Homeless (FEANTSA) recognises that the right to exit homelessness is the most important right of a homeless person. This implies that homeless individuals should have access to services that support their search for appropriate housing solutions.[47] Of course, this is another type of exit right, as in the typology developed in this paper, but it clearly shows that access, occupancy, and exit rights are closely interrelated.

6 CONCLUSION

The research on the scope, implementation, and effects of the right to adequate housing is flourishing. This paper proposes a typology that would serve as a useful tool to understand the research's outcomes. The typology provides a more conceptually sound research approach, prevents semantic confusion and miscommunication, and enables researchers to focus on specific dimensions of the right to adequate housing. Furthermore, it will facilitate a more systematic and comparative analysis of findings in national and regional projects focusing on the right to adequate housing. It is important to note that the boundaries between access, occupancy, and exit rights are not fixed. Rather, the typology is meant to be used as a hermeneutic tool for interpretation rather than as rigid categories into which every legal provision, judgement, opinion, or research project must fit perfectly. It is hoped that in the future, the typology will be further developed and compared with other categorisations, frameworks, and typologies, thereby enhancing the field of research on the right to adequate housing.

45 K. Amore, M. Baker & P. Howden-Chapman, 'The ETHOS Definition and Classification of Homelessness: An Analysis', European Journal of Homelessness, Vol. 5, No. 2, 2011, pp. 19-37.

46 P. Kenna et al. (Eds.), Loss of Homes and Evictions across Europe: A Comparative Legal and Policy Examination, Cheltenham, Edward Elgar Publishing, 2018; L. Slingenberg & L. Bonneau, '(In)Formal Migrant Settlements and Right to Respect for a Home', European Journal of Migration and Law, Vol. 19, No. 4, 2017, pp. 335-369; A. Flynn & E. van Wagner, 'Introduction to the Special Issue on Housing Precarity and Human Rights', Journal of Law and Social Policy, Vol. 36, 2023, pp. 1-11.

47 A. Ploszka, 'A Homeless Bill of Rights as a New Instrument to Protect the Rights of Homeless Persons', European Constitutional Law Review, Vol. 16, No. 4, 2020, pp. 601-624.

The Data Detectives: Examining the Impact of CESCR Case Law in a Housing Context

Andrei-Fabian Balan and Emma Bowar

1 Introduction

One of the main goals of the EVICT project is to determine to what extent the international right to housing prevents evictions. To this end, the various documents and decisions produced by the Committee on Economic, Social and Cultural Rights (hereinafter: the Committee) and relating to Article 11(1) of the International Covenant on Economic, Social and Cultural Rights (ICESCR) are currently being collected, systemised, and analysed. By creating such a database, we aim to provide a comprehensive overview of the Committee's approach to the right to housing as well as the State Parties' policy on housing and their relevant social support systems.

Article 11 ICESCR recognises, among others, the human right to adequate housing. The main task of the Committee – a body of eighteen independent experts – is to monitor the implementation of the ICESCR and to ensure that the right to housing is respected, protected, and fulfilled by the State Parties.[1] It does this by engaging in a dialogue with the State Parties, as well as by delivering quasi-judicial decisions on complaints brought before it by groups or individuals. Understanding the Committee's decisions is essential in this endeavour, as it is one of the main international mechanisms by which an individual may seek redress against eviction. As such, its decisions are partially indicative of the strength of the international right to housing.

2 Plan of Approach

We began by collecting and analysing the decisions of the Committee regarding the right to housing, focusing on the United Kingdom, Spain, and the Netherlands. In total, twenty-six complaints alleging a violation of an individual's right to housing have reached

1 UN Office of the High Commissioner for Human Rights (OHCHR), Fact Sheet No 21 (Rev. 1): The Human Right to Adequate Housing, 2009, p. 33.

the Committee, three of which have resulted in the Committee finding a violation of Article 11(1) ICESCR. All of these complaints have been filed against Spain, with the earliest complaint filed in 2015.

In analysing the complaints brought before the Committee, we assessed not only the decision the Committee ultimately reached but also examined whether children were involved as well as considering the extent to which additional treaties (other than the ICESCR) or the Committee's earlier case law were cited in the explanation of their decision. Following our analysis of the Committee's case law on the right to housing, we turned our attention to the State Parties' reports submitted to the Committee by Spain, the Netherlands, and the United Kingdom. A State Party's report is an assessment made by a State Party on the implementation of the various ICESCR rights within its domestic systems, intended to guide the Committee in its work. To ensure verifiable data, we drafted a codebook to guide our reading of the State Parties' reports. When writing the codebook, we aimed to define the variables as precisely as possible while at the same time ensuring we would capture all information related to the right to housing in the different state parties. Given that this database is one of the foundational elements of the EVICT project, we wanted to ensure we included all possibly relevant information for researchers later in the process to access. For example, our variables included an assessment of the extent to which, if at all, the State Parties' reports discussed the right to property in relation to the right to housing. Housing and property were given broad definitions to ensure that all the relevant information would be noted, but a limitation was placed on property insofar as it had to be immovable property. In this way, superfluous information would be avoided.

3 First Results

Concerning the Committee's case law on housing, we found that all twenty-six complaints had been directed against Spain. This might be explained by the fact that Spain is one of the few countries that has ratified the Optional Protocol to the International Covenant on Economic, Social and Cultural Rights, allowing the use of an individual complaint procedure for (groups of) citizens. Furthermore, we observed that violations of Article 11(1) were found only in 11.5% of all cases (as depicted in Figure 1), while the majority of the Committee cases were either discontinued or deemed inadmissible. This means that in a significant number of cases, the housing issues were resolved by the state before the end of the proceedings, the applicants could not be reached anymore (and, thus, the cases were consequently discontinued), or the applications failed to meet the admissibility requirements.

Figure 1 Decisions of the committee (N = 26).

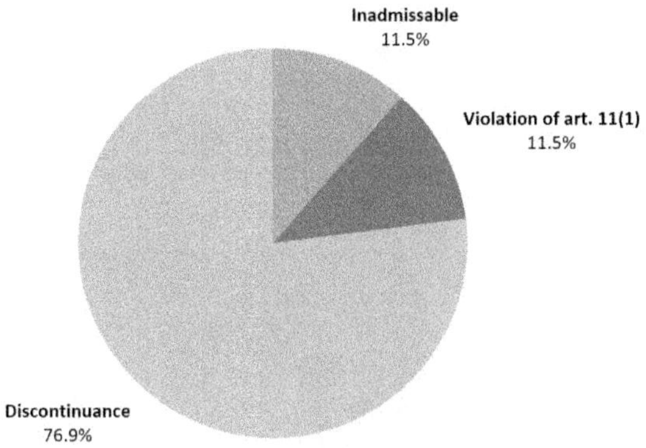

With regard to the State Parties reports, we have noticed that they were submitted seemingly arbitrarily in most cases. According to Article 16 of the ICESCR, each State Party must submit a report within two years after ratifying the Covenant and every five years after that. However, none of the State Parties we have analysed respected the aforementioned deadlines, causing reports to be submitted at widely varying dates, which can be observed in the following timeline (Figure 2).

Nevertheless, we noticed that the latest State Parties' reports contained a significant amount of information regarding (the right to) housing, evictions, and the predicament of various minorities with regard to housing. Some examples of such information found in the reports involve graphs and charts regarding the rates of homelessness and evictions, social programmes, and the housing situation of underprivileged groups of citizens. However, any information related to housing presented in the earliest State Parties reports was relatively scarce and succinct compared to the information found in the most recent reports.

4 CONCLUSION: THE ROAD AHEAD

Having collected and analysed the case law of the Committee concerning the right to housing and having studied the State Parties' reports of Spain, the UK, and the Netherlands, we will continue our research by focusing on the Lists of Issues and the Replies to the Lists of Issues produced by the Committee. Briefly summarised, these Lists of Issues represent questions posed by the Committee with the aim of obtaining more information on relevant issues in the State Parties. Furthermore, the Replies to the Lists of Issues are the responses sent by the State Parties in which they elaborate on how they plan to tackle the problems brought to their attention by the Committee. These issues are addressed, for example, by commencing an initiative to aid disadvantaged individuals, granting subsidies to social programmes, or increasing spending on infrastructure. Henceforth, we will continue to analyse the documents of the Committee in order to build a reliable database of pertinent information related to housing.

Figure 2 Screenshot of the timeline on the implementation of the ICESCR and the submission of reports by the UK, Spain, and the Netherlands, as required by Article 16 of the ICESCR. For the complete and interactive (online) version of the timeline, please scan the QR-code.

Part I
Access Rights

Introduction to Access Rights

Stefan van Tongeren

In the introduction of this book, access rights are explained as an individual's right to enter or secure housing through ownership, rental, or other means. Access rights play a vital role in addressing the marginalisation, stigmatisation, and exclusion of (minority) groups. They may offer legal protection against housing discrimination and help eliminate (other) social, economic, or physical barriers to housing. Access rights, moreover, require national governments to implement measures that ensure and promote the availability, affordability, and accessibility of decent housing for all.[1] Taken together, access rights provide any individual with a right to settle somewhere in peace, security, and dignity.[2]

The roots of access rights can be traced across numerous international and regional human rights documents, such as the Convention on the Rights of Persons with Disabilities, the International Convention on the Elimination of All Forms of Racial Discrimination, and the Convention on the Rights of the Child. On a European level, access rights can be found in the European Convention on Human Rights (ECHR) and the European Social Charter (ESC), as well as in a number of (legal) documents produced by the European Union. Yet, it is Article 11 of the International Covenant on Economic, Social and Cultural Rights (ICESCR) that can be considered one of the most significant legal sources on the right to adequate housing, and as such on access rights. States signatory to the ICESCR are obligated to "respect, protect and fulfil"[3] individuals' access rights and to undertake "whatever steps necessary"[4] to realise these rights.

The papers in this section of the book highlight several crucial dimensions concerning the availability of housing across various jurisdictions. The authors illustrate a range of challenges governments face when trying to ensure people's access to housing, yet also critically assess policies actively impeding the access rights of individuals and (minority) groups, thus exemplifying a gap between commitment and implementation.

---

1 UN Office of the High Commissioner for Human Rights (OHCHR), Fact Sheet No. 21 (Rev. 1), The Human Right to Adequate Housing, 2009, pp. 3-4. For examples of such measures implemented by various European countries, see The Foundation Abbé Pierre & FEANTSA, Eighth Overview of Housing Exclusion in Europe, Brussels, FEANTSA, 2023.

2 UN Committee on Economic, Social and Cultural Rights (CESCR), General Comment No. 4: The Right to Adequate Housing (Art. 11 (1) of the Covenant), 13 December 1991, E/1992/23, p. 7.

3 OHCHR, 2009, pp. 33-37.

4 CESCR, 1991, p. 11.

The first three papers examine how the policies of local authorities hinder the access rights of squatters and students, and showcase how a lack of government intervention places women experiencing domestic violence at risk of becoming homeless. The fourth paper critically examines the Swedish government's response to housing shortages, revealing flaws in the housing policy that contribute to the emergence of a black housing market. The last two papers explore the critical issue of homelessness, presenting two contrasting approaches: one, exemplified by the French DALO Law, which aims to provide homeless individuals with an enforceable right to housing; the other, seen in the Netherlands, which involves the criminalisation of homelessness through the use of area bans. These case studies collectively underscore the complexities and nuances of access rights, offering insights into both governmental shortcomings and innovative solutions in addressing housing challenges.

A Dive into the Parisian Housing Crisis: Squatters' Rights, Abandoned Properties, and Questionable Legislation

Gabriel Osinga

1 Introduction

As the world's population edges ever closer to the eight billion mark, a new dynamic has formed between humans and housing. This increase in population has seen a dramatic upshift in demand for accommodation which has created a strain on the housing market. As such, worldwide affordable housing shortages[1] have appeared and have contributed, together with an ever-extortionate cost of living due to inflation,[2] to elevated amounts of homelessness.

This can most notably be seen in major cities, such as Paris, where the immensely high cost of living can be largely attributed to the real estate market. In 1999, the average price per square metre was between 1,790 and 4,120 euros, whereas these figures have increased to between 6,920 and 12,200 euros in 2016.[3] Accordingly, affordability has worsened as Parisian property value has increased by 70% from 2000 to 2019.[4] This has resulted in over 30,000 people being homeless in the capital city alone.[5]

---

1 S. Crowley, 'The Affordable Housing Crisis: Residential Mobility of Poor Families and School Mobility of Poor Children', The Journal of Negro Education, Vol. 72, No. 1, 2003, pp. 22-38.

2 A.C. Karantonis, 'Population Growth and Housing Affordability in the Modern City – Sydney a Case Study', 4th Pacific Rim Real Estate Society Conference, 2008, pp. 1-16.

3 Paris Property Group, 'How Has the Price of Paris Real Estate Evolved over Time?', Paris Property Group, https://parispropertygroup.com/blog/2017/how-paris-real-estate-prices-evolved/ (last accessed 3 August 2023).

4 Inspection Générale de l'Environnement et du Développement durable (IGEDD), Property Price and Rent History, 1936-2023 in France and 1200-2023 in Paris: Statistics and Analyses', IGEDD, https://www.igedd.developpement-durable.gouv.fr/house-prices-in-france-property-price-index-french-a1117.html (last accessed 3 August 2023).

5 G. Daly, Homeless, New York, Routledge, 1996.

2 Covid-19

Another notable contribution to Paris's homelessness crisis has been the impact of Covid-19. The virus has had a significant impact on unemployment rates, and it has been estimated that this has reached 8.6% in France in 2020.[6] Thus, this has had, and will undoubtedly have, a significant impact on homelessness as this would create difficulties in people's ability to pay rent due to their lack of income. However, what is astonishing is that as of September 2020, it has been reported that about 15% of Parisian properties remain unoccupied.[7] This has been a growing issue in the nation's capital for some time and has actually become more severe over time, as this number was 'only' down to 7.5% in 2017.[8] The city has been fighting this issue for years in a quest to minimise wasted properties. In 1998, the 'Taxe sur les Logements Vacants' (Tax on Vacant Lodgements) was introduced, and in 2017, the Paris Council amended Article 1407 ter of the 'Code général des impôts' (General Tax Code), which increased taxes for unoccupied and second homes. This increase saw taxes for these properties increase from 20% to 60% in a bid to incentivise property owners,[9] much like the 1998 'Taxe sur les Logements Vacants' (TLV) law,[10] to sell off unused properties and contribute to the housing market. However, as the figures demonstrate, this has been an uphill battle for the Paris Council and one that they are losing. Vacancies have continued to increase, and it seems as if legislative efforts have not successfully reversed this trend. Cumulatively, the factors of a housing market unable to keep up with the demands of an ever-growing population, the increasing cost of living, elevated unemployment, and the large number of unoccupied properties have led some of the economically unstable Parisians to attempt to obtain a home through less conventional methods, for instance by means of squatting.

3 Squatting

Squatting is the act of unlawfully penetrating an apartment or building in which the person who has a title to the building has terminated or simply not given permission to

6 G. Dib, K. Utermühl & J. Junge, 30 million Unemployed Go Missing and with Them USD14BN of Monthly Consumption, Munich, Allianz Research, 2020.

7 VICE, 'Inside Paris' Illegal Squats', VICE, 29 March 2021, https://www.youtube.com/watch?v=KjskPRXeZjg&ab_channel=VICE (last accessed 3 August 2023).

8 Better Dwelling, 'Vacant Homes Are a Global Epidemic, and Paris Is Fighting It with a 60% Tax', Better Dwelling, 2 March 2017, https://betterdwelling.com/vacant-homes-global-epidemic-paris-fighting-60-tax/ (last accessed 3 August 2023).

9 Ibid.

10 M. Segú & B. Vignolles, 'Taxing Vacant Apartments: Can Fiscal Policy Reduce Vacancy?', International Network for Economic Research (INFER), 2016.

use it.[11] This method of obtaining housing has been used for a long time by 'squatters' and has even resulted in the creation of iconic parts of the city of Paris. For example, in 1999, a group of squatter artists occupied 59 Rue de Rivoli and transformed it into what is now known as 'Rivoli 59', serving as a famous art gallery which attracts 70,000 visitors every year.[12] The iconic image of Rivoli 59 meant that in 2006, the Parisian city hall bought the space and legislation was introduced in order to make it a legal entity with application processes and monthly fees. This has divided the squatting community,[13] as some members of Rivoli 59 welcome the legislation as it legitimises their residence and is a more advantageous situation as they do not get evicted after a certain amount of time. However, others believe that the city criminalises the act of squatting in some instances whilst at the same time contrarily legalising certain squats which they deem presentable. Thus, squats have developed from a mere shelter to a cultural identity with a history behind them,[14] as exemplified by the thirty artists residing within the Rivoli 59 squat. Irrespective of one's view on the process of legalising the Rivoli 59 squat, it is clear that the squat itself has had a positive impact on the community. However, this still does not address the issue that many properties are still left unoccupied and unused whilst Paris's homelessness crisis worsens.

It seems as if many of these properties could be used to accommodate people experiencing homelessness and be transformed into squats. To an extent, this idea has gained traction throughout the community, as vacant properties awaiting construction, termed 'meanwhile spaces', have been transformed throughout the city into temporary urban campsites up until construction recommences. This initiative has revived empty properties and essentially revived these abandoned locations for the benefit of the community as well as acting as a clever solution to the French capital's problem. Of these 'meanwhile spaces', some have seen great success and have even experienced high tourist activity akin to Rivoli 59. In 2015, formerly home to the Saint-Vincent-de-Paul hospital, a property in Paris's 14th district was transformed into house allotments called 'Les Grands Voisins' with a football pitch and even a market.[15] It created a community

11 H. Pruijt, 'Culture Wars, Revanchism, Moral Panics and the Creative City. A Reconstruction of a Decline of Tolerant Public Policy: The Case of Dutch Anti-squatting Legislation', Urban Studies, Vol. 50, No. 6, 2012, pp. 1114-1129.

12 See their website: www.59rivoli.org/homepage/

13 T. Aguilera, 'The Squatting Movement(s) in Paris: Internal Divides and Conditions for Survival', in M.A. Martínez López (Ed.), The Urban Politics of Squatters' Movements, New York, Palgrave Macmillan, 2018, pp. 121-144.; P. Yeung, 'Paris Is Killing Its Art Squats to Gentrify the City', Dazed, 11 October 2019, https://www.dazeddigital.com/life-culture/article/46369/1/paris-is-killing-its-artist-squats-to-gentrify-the-city (last accessed 3 August 2023).

14 Squatting Europe Kollective, Squatting in Europe: Radical Spaces, Urban Struggles, Brooklyn, Minor Compositions, 2013.

15 L. Latham, 'The Rise of the 'Meanwhile Space': How Empty Properties Are Finding Second Lives', The Guardian, 28 November 2018, https://www.theguardian.com/cities/2018/nov/28/the-rise-of-the-meanwhile-space-how-empty-properties-are-finding-second-lives (last accessed 3 August 2023).

and established a relationship between residents and shoppers alike which proved beneficial to all. As the property was scheduled for reconstruction in 2020, the empty space was put to use to accommodate over 2,000 workers and residents. Construction of a new neighbourhood commenced in 2020, and as such, Les Grands Voisins is permanently closed. However, during the period that it was open, it demonstrated a creative solution to Paris's housing and empty property issues.

Despite the success of Rivoli 59 and Les Grands Voisins, they are placed on the extremely positive end of a spectrum, which, as can be deduced, contains many less successful instances of squatting. InfoMigrants, an online project funded by the EU and led by major European news agencies such as Deutsche Welle, France Medias Monde, and ANSA, reported in 2021 on a disused Parisian office which held 250 migrants in January.[16] It outlines the struggles the migrants have with obtaining food, water, and warmth as it recounts a crowd forming around an aid organisation's van as they opened their doors to give out blankets and food. It describes the makeshift home as having "broken window frames, smashed up windows patched up with cardboard, leaking pipes, visible grime, broken toilets, no showers".[17] The article further recalls that firefighters were called twice during InfoMigrants' visit on January 26 as occupants of the building had injured themselves on the unsafe stairs of the premises. Clearly, squatting is still an issue in the city, and it shows that legislative support is needed in order to better accommodate people experiencing homelessness.

Even with initiatives such as Rivoli 59 and Les Grands Voisins, the issue of abandoned and unused buildings, in combination with the lack of housing for many, still looms large in Paris and for that matter, within the whole of Europe. In reality, steps have even been taken in order to make it harder for squatters to have shelter, and laws have been passed by the French government, which give property owners more power.

The introduction of stricter squatting legislation into the French legal system came as a response to many instances in which property was damaged by squatters who had taken over the premises. Notably, in 2020, owners of a house in Théole-sur-Mer were forced to deep clean and even replace furniture and walls after squatters had used the home as a temporary abode. Although not located in Paris, it highlighted an issue that arises when squatters enter properties and use them for themselves without permission from the owner, and it has been a contributing factor to the stricter legislation that France has implemented and proposed over the 2020-2021 period.

---

16 C. Oberti, "We Do What the State Doesn't Do': Surviving a Paris Squat Filled with Tents', InfoMigrants, 3 February 2021, https://www.infomigrants.net/en/post/29952/we-do-what-the-state-doesnt-do-surviving-a-paris-squat-filled-with-tents (last accessed 3 August 2023).

17 Ibid.

4 Eviction Proceedings

Previously, owners of properties inhabited by squatters would have to commence judicial proceedings to evict them if the squatters were discovered after forty-eight hours of entering the premises.[18] This process could take weeks or even months before a court decision was reached.[19] Thus, even if the court decided in favour of the property owner, the squatters would still have shelter for the weeks or months leading up to the final decision. However, the French government introduced a new law in November 2020 which removed the forty-eight-hour limit and instead made it possible for owners to complain as soon as they found out that there were intruders on their property. Additionally, the law prescribes that in case the police cannot move the squatters, owners can apply to the prefect of the police department, who must respond within forty-eight hours as to whether they can or cannot remove the squatters by force. If the department refuses to do so, they must also provide justification for this.[20] This law drastically reduces the time it takes to remove squatters from properties in many instances and takes away the lengthy judicial process that squatters have relied upon to maintain shelter.

Consequently, the introduction of this law has sparked controversy from both human rights and property-owners-rights activists. The law can be seen as an obstacle to potential squatters' right to life contained in Article 2 of the European Convention on Human Rights (ECHR), their right to respect for private and family life in Article 8 ECHR, and their right to security in Article 5 ECHR. Simultaneously, though, it has the possibility of still not protecting property owners adequately, as the law does not have any effect on evicting squatters in situations where the prefect has refused to take action. As such, many property owners believe their property rights are being infringed upon. Lawyers in France have also argued that the requirement that the prefect provides justification for refusals to act is ineffective in practice as the prefect's reasoning can be extremely vague as the law provides that the prefect can justify the decision to not move the squatters by merely stating that it would cause a threat to public order.[21] One can easily deduce how this term has the possibility of being used in many situations due to its very broad and far-reaching nature.

---

18 French-Property.com, 'Removing Squatters from Your French Property', French-Property.com, 6 July 2021, https://www.french-property.com/news/french_property/eviction_squatters_new_law#:~:text=The%20French%20government%20have%20strengthened,squatters%20without%20a%20court%20order (last accessed 3 August 2023).

19 VICE, 2021.

20 The Connexion, 'France's New Anti-squatter Laws Will Be "Hard to Implement"', The Connexion, 11 March 2021, https://www.connexionfrance.com/article/Practical/Property/France-s-new-anti-squatter-laws-will-be-hard-to-implement (last accessed 3 August 2023).

21 R.R. Landi, 'Comment expulser un squatteur?', Rossi-Landi Avocats, https://rossi-landi-avocats.fr/publication/comment-expulser-un-squatteur/ (last accessed 3 August 2023).

It is additionally argued that these laws revolve around safety as many of the buildings that squatters occupy have been abandoned in the first place for not meeting modern safety requirements, such as possessing acceptable fire escapes or having weak foundations.[22] In a sense, it could be argued that the restrictions on using these properties as *de facto* shelter are indeed to uphold the right to life in Article 2 ECHR, but many squatters believe that this view possesses a major flaw in the sense that most people would rather live in an 'unsafe' building complex than in the street.

5 Conclusion

The implementation of stricter legislation for squatting rights creates more issues than it resolves. Their implementation as a response to squatters damaging properties and the need for property-owners is not by its merits unjust, but the negative effect heavily outweighs the positive. The trend to implement stricter laws only contributes to Paris's (and France's) homelessness crisis as it makes it much easier to force squatters back on the street with no protection from the elements and other societal dangers that one can extrapolate would be present on the city streets. Further, the properties used for squatting are implicitly unoccupied or abandoned (otherwise, it would be impossible for the squatters to take over the property in the first place). Thus, an increase in the ease with which it is possible to force squatters off properties has the effect of elevating the already substantial amount of abandoned and unused properties in Paris. Somewhat paradoxically, this is clearly an issue that troubles the French and Parisian governments since, as previously mentioned, they have introduced elevated taxes to counter vacant properties. Additionally, and at the core of the issue, it contributes to the inability of France's housing market to adequately accommodate a considerable population and consequently means that many individuals experience infringements on their rights contained within the European Convention on Human Rights.

A more suitable approach to tackle this issue would be to further legitimise the use of abandoned or unused property as squatting locations through more legislation. As seen through Rivoli 59 and Les Grands Voisins, this can have a positive impact on multiple levels. Such legislation would most likely add regulation and quasi-institutionalisation to squatting and could even create task forces which would deal with ensuring that unused properties are as safe as they can be. Further, regulations that include a lower threshold for safety requirements of abandoned buildings could be passed, thus allowing more squatters to use buildings legally. Building on the idea of the increased tax on unused second properties, rules could be implemented which allow squatters

22 VICE, 2021.

to temporarily use the property legally until the owner needs the premise again if that original property owner has not done so themselves after a certain period of time. This would allow squatters to make use of unused properties whilst striking a balance with property owners' rights as they would regain control of the property once they need it again. Of course, this issue is extremely complicated, and it seems as if it is far from being resolved. As initiatives and legalisation of certain squats continue to increase, stricter legislative proposals regarding squatter rights also experience a similar trend. As the French government struggles to strike a fair balance between property owners' and squatters' rights through these means, the cost of living and, in turn, the homeless population in Paris continues to increase at an unprecedented scale. Given the circumstances at the time of writing this paper in mid-2021, it is clear that an effective remedy, and a quick one at that, is needed before this issue spirals into an even more uncontrollable state.

The Students of Groningen: Homeless and Hopeless in the Midst of a Housing Crisis

Maria Niemelä

1 Introduction

Nearing the beginning of the new academic year, the Dutch city of Groningen (famously known as a student city) had warned students not to come if they had not secured a place to stay.[1] In 2021, the city saw a lot of students experiencing homelessness. According to Shelter Our Students (SOS), an emergency couch-surfing platform based in Groningen,[2] around 600 students reached out to get help last year.[3] Six months later, some remained unable to find a home.[4]

2 A Student City in Need of Student Housing

Groningen has been nicknamed one of the youngest cities in Europe. It is no surprise as the city is home to two major educational institutions, the University of Groningen and Hanze University of Applied Sciences. Together, the schools host 60,000 students, accounting for 25% of the city's total population.[5] Although it presents itself as a student city, the city has not been able to accommodate the ever-increasing number of students. In 2021, many found themselves sleeping in rows of beds located in tents and being

1 Gemeente Groningen, 'Housing Foreign Students', Gemeente Groningen, https://gemeente.groningen.nl/en/housing-foreign-students (last accessed 1 August 2023).

2 For more information on S.O.S., see their website: www.sosgroningen.nl (last accessed 1 August 2023).

3 NL Times, 'Hundreds of International Students Homeless in Groningen', NL Times, 8 September 2021, https://nltimes.nl/2021/09/08/hundreds-international-students-homeless-groningen (last accessed 1 August 2023).

4 C. Schwaiger et al., 'Faces of Homelessness: Six Months on & Still No Room', UKrant, 9 February 2021, https://ukrant.nl/magazine/faces-of-homelessness-six-months-on-and-these-students-still-dont-have-a-room/?lang=en (last accessed 1 August 2023).

5 Groningen.nl, 'Groningen: Student City', Groningen.nl, https://groningen.nl/en/study/discover-student-life/groningen-student-city (last accessed 1 August 2023).

charged 12.50 euros per night.[6] The effects of tenure insecurity and the lack of adequate space are reflected in low educational achievements during a period in life that is particularly important for shaping one's future.

Unlike some universities abroad, campus and dorm accommodation services offered by the universities in Groningen are few and far between in the country.[7] Students are themselves responsible for finding accommodation. However, this can prove challenging as Groningen's housing market is plagued by a severe undersupply with an estimated shortage of 7,400 houses, making it a daunting task to find affordable housing.[8] Students in particular may have difficulty keeping up with the competitive prices of the rental market because they often lack their own income. For example, a recent advertisement listed a small bedroom (approximately 3m × 5m in area, with limited space due to a slanted ceiling) on the city's outskirts for 695 euros a month, with a bathroom shared with two other tenants.[9] It is truly a landlord's market.

Students' chances of finding housing are further hampered by indirect efforts, such as the various requirements imposed by sceptical landlords to exclude students from the application process at the outset. These include requirements for income, guarantor, and lease history.[10] Language requirements, common to shared accommodation, pose an additional challenge for international students.[11] Some have gone to the point of declaring 'no internationals' in their advertisements.[12]

---

6 E. Brown, '5 Things to Know about the Dutch Student Housing Crisis', Dutch Review, 24 August 2022, https://dutchreview.com/expat/housing/renting/student-housing-crisis-in-the-netherlands/ (last accessed 1 August 2023).

7 J.G. Kiewiet, The Different Types of Student Residences in the City of Groningen; How Do These Influence the Well-Being of Students? Groningen, University of Groningen, 2022.

8 The Northern Times, 'Groningen Housing Shortage to Rise to 10,000 Homes by 2025', The Northern Times, 22 February 2022, https://northerntimes.nl/groningen-housing-shortage-projected-to-rise-to-10000-homes-by-2025/ (last accessed 1 August 2023).

9 W. Groeneveld, 'Hyena vraagt 695 euro voor kleine klotenkamer in Lewenborg: "De luxe badkamer deel je met 2 anderen"', Sikkom, 28 August 2022, https://www.sikkom.nl/actueel/Hyena-vraagt-695-euro-voor-kleine-klotenkamer-in-Lewenborg-%E2%80%9CDe-luxe-badkamer-deel-je-met-2-anderen%E2%80%9D-27983936.html (last accessed 1 August 2023).

10 K. Broton & S. Goldrick-Rab, 'Housing Instability among College Students', Center for Financial Security, Madison, University of Wisconsin, 2013.

11 S. Smith et al., 'The Right to Adequate Housing in the Context of International Education', Australian International Education Conference Paper, 2007.

12 A. Tessari, 'Sorry, No Internationals', UKrant, 22 June 2022, https://ukrant.nl/magazine/sorry-no-internationals-alleen-nederlanders-krijgen-een-kamer/ (last accessed 23 August 2023).

3 Groningen: an Example of the Dutch Student Housing Crisis

The housing situation of students in the Netherlands is a social problem. Similar reports of students on the streets have surfaced in Utrecht, Maastricht, and Amsterdam.[13] Ultimately, the problem can be pinpointed to two major factors – the housing shortage and the fact that universities are taking in too many (international) students. To address the concerns of an increasing international student population, possible solutions that have been identified so far include reducing the number of English study programmes and communicating with international students more effectively to adequately inform them of the housing situation in the Netherlands.[14]

4 Conclusion

Some progress has been made in Groningen following the eight-hour occupation of the University of Groningen academy building by SOS. in September 2021.[15] As a consequence of the event, the University of Groningen, Hanze University of Applied Sciences, and the municipality agreed to increase the availability of emergency housing, lower the prices per night, and communicate more clearly with incoming students. For the academic year 2023/2024, the University has set out to construct 400 temporary rooms on campus for the next 15 years.[16] This would relieve the pressure on lengthy construction projects as a solution to the housing shortage. Yet, this is still no solution to the housing shortage for the upcoming academic year. Time will tell how big the issue will be for students this year.

13 X. van Uffelen, 'Tekort aan kamers loopt snel op door grote aanwas van buitenlandse studenten', Volkskrant, 8 September 2022, https://www.universityworldnews.com/post.php?story=20220619083123474 (last accessed 6 March 2024).

14 British Universities' International Liaison Association (BUILA), 'Universities Warn Students Not to Travel Amid Housing Shortages', BUILA, 19 August 2022, https://www.buila.ac.uk/news/2022/universities-warn-students-not-to-travel-amid-housing-shortages (last accessed 1 August 2023).

15 G. Fabrizi, 'UG and City Close Deal with Protesters after They Occupied Academy Building', UKrant, 10 September 2021, https://ukrant.nl/ug-and-city-close-deal-with-protesters-after-they-occupied-academy-building/?lang=en (last accessed 1 August 2023).

16 G. Fabrizi, 'Emergency Housing Hard to Arrange, City Worried about Homeless Students Once More', UKrant, 17 May 2022, https://ukrant.nl/emergency-housing-hard-to-arrange-city-worried-about-homeless-students-once-more/?lang=en (last accessed 1 August 2023).

Housing Behind Law's Back: Sweden's Acute Housing Shortage and the Looming Black Market

Maria Niemelä

1 Introduction

The right to adequate housing in Sweden is a constitutionally recognised 'allmännytta': a right that belongs to everyone in the country and is protected as such.[1] This means that all tenures are considered equal, which is reflected in the lack of social housing. Instead of protecting only a part of the population through subsidised apartments, the Swedish system aims to offer affordable quality housing for all. The responsibility to ensure housing for everyone lies with the 290 municipalities, out of which 255 report a housing shortage.[2] This has several reasons. Compared to other European Union countries, Sweden's homeownership rate is relatively low at 64.9%,[3] marking the rental housing market as substantial but difficult to access for lower-income households.[4] Purchasing housing is out of the question for the socially disadvantaged, such as immigrants, addicts, and those who suffer from mental health issues. Moreover, those lucky enough to find housing hold onto it for their dear lives or sublet it for profits in illegal contracts which offer tenants little to no legal protection.[5] Lastly and more fundamentally, much of the needed housing simply does not physically exist – according to an estimation by Sweden's National Board of Housing, the capital Stockholm would have to build

1 Sveriges Allmännytta, 'Allmännyttan', Sveriges Allmännytta, https://www.sverigesallmannytta.se/allmannyttan/ (last accessed 1 August 2023).

2 L. Roden, 'The Story of Sweden's Housing Crisis', The Local, 28 August 2017, https://www.thelocal.se/20170828/the-story-of-swedens-housing-crisis (last accessed 1 August 2023).

3 Eurostat, 'Distribution of Population by Tenure Status, Type of Household and Income Group – EU-SILC Survey', Eurostat, https://ec.europa.eu/eurostat/databrowser/view/ILC_LVHO02__custom_3553007/bookmark/table?lang=en&bookmarkId=2457e44e-df35-4995-aacc-e79684402691 (last accessed 1 August 2023).

4 A.G. Hansson, 'Housing the Vulnerable: Municipal Strategies in the Swedish Housing Regime', European Journal of Homelessness, Vol. 15, No. 2, 2021, pp. 13-36.

5 Austrian Economics Center, 'Rent Control Has Failed in Sweden', Austrian Economics Center, 24 January 2020, https://austriancenter.com/rent-control-has-failed-in-sweden/ (last accessed 1 August 2023).

approximately 25,000 to 30,000 homes a year in order to meet the pressing demand.[6] These issues raise questions about whether the ideology behind the housing policy is serving the current reality.

2 Flaws in the Current Swedish Housing Policy

There are two important mechanisms to ensure the two core values, equality and affordability, in the Swedish housing provision system. However, they do not come without issues. One is employed in the application process for rental apartments – the municipality's apartment waiting list for public housing. There is no prioritisation of applicants based on their housing needs, making all housing options available to everyone, regardless of their social class. While the system is seemingly equal, it can easily be taken advantage of by the financially secure classes, who may then occupy the affordable, well-located apartments. As a result, the vulnerable groups are pushed to the outskirts of the city, harming the (re)integration process of some into society.[7] The waiting list concretises the pure lack of housing – the average queuing time in the capital ranges from nine to sixteen years.

The second mechanism primarily concerns the private sector, which makes up half of the rental housing market.[8] It works to achieve affordability in urban areas and is known as the 'bruksvärdessystem' – the utility value system.[9] Instead of allowing the market forces to regulate prices, the Swedish Union of Tenants performs an estimate of the value of a dwelling based on its characteristics and utilities. As such, the procedure acts as a price ceiling, preventing private landlords from making an excessive profit while ensuring that both public and private sectors compete for the same share of tenants.

Although the 'bruksvärdessystem' is seemingly effective in its quest for affordability, it is also a key contributor to the lengthy housing queue in the city, leading many to resort

---

6 Reuters, 'FACTBOX-Dysfunctional Swedish Housing Market behind Ouster of PM Lofven', Reuters, 23 June 2021, https://www.reuters.com/article/sweden-housing-idUSL5N2O51RM (last accessed 1 August 2023).

7 A.S. Nissanka, Beyond a Roof and Walls: Gaps and Challenges in Providing Adequate Housing for Refugees in Malmö, Malmö, Malmö University, 2020.

8 Housing Europe, 'Public Housing Sweden: Formerly SABO', Housing Europe, https://www.housingeurope.eu/member-57/public-housing-sweden (last accessed 1 August 2023).

9 M. Baléo, 'Stockholm: A Universalist Vision of Housing Tested by Shortages', La Fabrique de la Cité, 4 June 2019, https://www.lafabriquedelacite.com/en/publications/stockholm-a-universalist-vision-of-housing-tested-by-shortages/ (last accessed 1 August 2023).

to black market housing.[10] It goes without saying that this 'off-the-books approach' is profitable to private landlords, who receive no monetary aid from municipalities, despite the essentially profit-limiting procedure. Furthermore, this may discourage investments[11] in building new housing in a country where it is already much pricier[12] compared to its neighbours in the European Union. Evaluation based on utility fails to take into account the subjective attractiveness of an apartment and can, therefore, even lead to underappreciation of its value, casting doubt on how well the reality is reflected in the 'bruksvärdessystem'.

3 Conclusion

As illustrated, the Swedish housing provision system seems unable to fulfil current housing needs, let alone protect vulnerable groups in the absence of state measures. However, many remain reluctant to the winds of change. In June, the left party withdrew support from Prime Minister Stefan Löfven, following plans to change the housing policy.[13] This led to the first-ever successful vote of no confidence in Sweden. Whether state intervention would imply a shift of model to one that supports social housing or one that merely provides a change of perspective, it is clear that the Swedish principle of 'housing for all' cannot exist in a time where the group of vulnerable people is growing. A real 'housing for all'-principle should specifically address the vulnerable to prevent the principle from turning into 'housing for the rich'.

10 M. Savage, 'Why Rent Control Isn't Working in Sweden', BBC, 26 August 2021, https://www.bbc.com/news/business-58317555 (last accessed 1 August 2023).

11 F. Bwanika, 'To What Extent Has the Utility Value System in Sweden Together with Other Economics Factors; Government Intervention, Interest Rates and Population Growth Affected the Housing Market in Stockholm', Academia, https://www.academia.edu/28395958/To_what_extent_has_the_Utility_Value_system_in_Sweden_together_with_other_economics_factors_government_intervention_interest_rates_and_population_growth_affected_the_housing_market_in_Stockholm?email_work_card=view-paper (last accessed 1 August 2023).

12 P.T. Finnson, 'What Explains the Extraordinary Increase in Swedish House Prices?', Nordregio Magazine, https://nordregio.org/nordregio-magazine/issues/nordic-housing-markets-and-policies/what-explains-the-extraordinary-increase-in-swedish-house-prices/ (last accessed 1 August 2023).

13 C. Duxbury, 'Swedish PM Faces No-confidence Vote after Clash over Rent Controls', Politico, 17 June 2021, https://www.politico.eu/article/sweden-prime-minister-stefan-lofven-government-no-confidence-vote-rent-controls/ (last accessed 1 August 2023).

Pathway to Homelessness: Analysing the Relationship between Domestic Violence and Housing Rights

Matleena Gurara

1 Introduction

The issue of domestic violence is a significant and widespread one, which affects society as a whole. The term 'domestic violence' implies a pattern of behaviour in any relationship that is used to gain or maintain power and control over an intimate partner.[1] It is important to stress that domestic violence can occur in a variety of settings including, but not limited to, child-parent, in-laws and LGBTQ+ relationships. In other words, it can take place within a range of relationships including couples who are married, living together or dating, and can affect people of all socioeconomic backgrounds and education levels. Simultaneously, both women and men can be victims or perpetrators of domestic violence. However, in this paper, specific focus will be given to the relationship between housing rights and abuse in the form of sexual, physical, emotional, psychological, or economic threats or actions perpetrated by male partners against their female partners.

2 Domestic Violence: Numbers and Figures in a Housing Rights Context

Although domestic violence constitutes only one of the multitude of expressions of violence[2] to which women are exposed, it is one of the most omnipresent manifestations of violence.[3] Even though data collection in this field is still underdeveloped, the

1 United Nations, 'What Is Domestic Abuse?', United Nations, https://www.un.org/en/coronavirus/what-is-domestic-abuse (last accessed 31 July 2023).
2 UN General Assembly, Declaration on the Elimination of Violence against Women, 20 December 1993, A/RES/48/104.
3 United Nations Department of Public Information, 'Violence against Women', United Nations Department of Public Information, May 2000, https://www.un.org/womenwatch/daw/followup/session/presskit/fs4.htm (last accessed 31 July 2023).

available statistics portray a grim picture. The following segment is taken from the 2006 study *Combating Violence against Women* by the Council of Europe:

> [A]n overview suggests that across countries, one-fifth to one-quarter of all women have experienced physical violence at least once during their adult lives, and more than one-tenth have suffered sexual violence involving the use of force. Figures for all forms of violence, including stalking, are as high as 45%.[4]

Furthermore, concerning domestic violence,

> [s]econdary data analyses … support an estimate that about 12% to 15% of all women have been in a relationship of domestic abuse after the age of 16. Rates of physical and sexual violence by former partners after separation are substantially higher, indicating that the protection of women is not secured when they end an abusive relationship.[5]

In the context of housing rights, approximately 50% to 60% of all homeless women report that they are homeless because they are fleeing domestic violence. The issue of those fleeing domestic violence does not easily fit into the definition of eviction, yet it does involve dispossession of the home. In several countries, research findings demonstrate that the percentage of homeless women who have experienced domestic violence extends up to 40% in the UK and Ireland to 50% in Portugal and Hungary, with an acutely higher proportion of partner abuse of 100% and 93% in Spain and Sweden respectively.[6] For instance, in the United Kingdom, Government figures show that in the year 2019, almost 24,000 people were made homeless directly because of domestic abuse.[7] Further, in the United States, half of all homeless women and children are fleeing abuse.[8]

---

4 C. Hagemann-White, Combating Violence against Woman: Stocktaking study on the measures and actions taken in Council of Europe member States, Strasbourg, Directorate General of Human Rights, Council of Europe, 2006, p. 7.

5 Ibid., p. 8.

6 FEANTSA, 'Women Experiencing Violence and Homelessness: Interlinked and Unaddressed Gender Specific Needs', FEANTSA, https://www.feantsa.org/public/user/Resources/Position_papers/FEANTSA_background_paper_Women%27s_Homelessness_and_GBV.pdf (last accessed 31 July 2023).

7 See the UK Government's Statutory homelessness live tables via https://www.gov.uk/government/statistical-data-sets/live-tables-on-homelessness (under 'Statutory homelessness in England'; last accessed 31 July 2023).

8 E.L. Bassuk et al., 'The Characteristics and Needs of Sheltered Homeless and Low-income Housed Mothers', The Journal of the American Medical Association, Vol. 276, No. 8, 1996, pp. 640-646.

Even though domestic violence certainly is an imperative and consequential factor in women's homelessness, it must be pointed out that homelessness and housing exclusion is a consequence of a tangled interaction between structural, systemic, and individual factors. Accordingly, policymakers recognise that factors such as poverty, housing market conditions, and mental illnesses can also impact the process of becoming homeless.[9] Thus, domestic violence leading up to homelessness extends across and is affected by broader phenomena of inequalities, social exclusion, and marginalisation of women present in many countries. While international and national laws increasingly recognise women's right to adequate housing, significant gaps remain between this recognition and the reality of widespread denial of this right.

3 What Progress Have International Institutions Made in Tackling This Problem?

At the United Nations level, the relationship between the right to housing and domestic violence was overlooked for a long time. The right to housing is affirmed in Article 25(1) of the Universal Declaration of Human Rights. Under that Article, everyone has the right to a standard of living adequate for the health and well-being of him- or herself and his or her family, including housing. This right is also repeated in Article 11(1) of the International Covenant on Economic, Social and Cultural Rights (hereafter: ICESCR). Due to its legally binding nature and as a result of various observations produced by the Committee on Economic, Social and Cultural Rights (hereafter: CESCR) on the essence of the right to housing under the ICESCR, Article 11(1) ICESCR is generally accepted as one of the most significant legal sources of this right. However, General Comment No. 4[10] of the CESCR, pertaining to the right under Article 11(1) ICESCR and being the most prominent explanatory document of the CESCR on the right to housing, is gender-neutral in all respects and does not acknowledge the dissimilarities between men and women in encountering the right to housing. In other words, General Comment No. 4 does not address the intricacies of women's right to housing, such as the extent to which women's housing rights are violated and the extent to which women are vulnerable to abuse within the home. Eventually, through Resolution 2000/9, the United Nations Commission on Human Rights appointed its first Special Rapporteur on adequate housing with a mandate to focus on adequate housing as a component of the right to an adequate standard of living in the context of non-discrimination.

9 G. Johnson et al., Examining the Relationship between Structural Factors, Individual Characteristics, and Homelessness, AHURI Positioning Paper No. 161, Melbourne, Australian Housing and Urban Research Institute, 2015.

10 UN Committee on Economic, Social and Cultural Rights (CESCR), General Comment No. 4: The Right to Adequate Housing (Art. 11 (1) of the Covenant), 13 December 1991, E/1992/23.

Accordingly, testimonies collected by the UN Special Rapporteur on adequate housing Miloon Kothari have highlighted the close link between domestic violence and women's right to adequate housing.[11] His successor, Leilani Farha, continued the same stance.[12]

Moreover, the Council of Europe has acknowledged the issue of domestic violence. For instance, the European Court of Human Rights (hereafter: the ECtHR) has stated in the case of *Opuz v. Turkey* that it

> can take various forms ranging from physical to psychological violence or verbal abuse…. It is a general problem that concerns all member States and which does not always surface since it often takes place within personal relationships or closed circuits and it is not only women who are affected. The ECtHR acknowledges that men may also be the victims of domestic violence and, indeed, that children, too, are often casualties of the phenomenon, whether directly or indirectly….[13]

In the same judgement, the ECtHR held that Turkey had violated Article 14 read in conjunction with Article 2 and Article 3 of the European Convention of Human Rights (hereafter: ECHR) on account of the violence suffered by the applicant and her mother having been gender-based, which amounted to a form of discrimination against women. Even though the applicant did not rely on Article 8 ECHR or Article 1 of Protocol No. 1 to the ECHR in her complaint, several references in the judgement indicate that the applicant was forced to leave her home due to threats by her husband. Later, in *Kalucza v. Hungary*, the ECtHR found a violation of Article 8 ECHR since Hungary failed to protect the applicant from an abusive partner despite repeated requests to have him evicted from their shared flat.[14] Additionally, the Commissioner for Human Rights of the Council of Europe has recommended that the Member States adopt anti-violence provisions in housing legislation and policies and ensure that domestic violence laws include provisions to protect women's right to housing.[15]

---

11 M. Koothrani, Women and Adequate Housing. Study by the Special Rapporteur on Adequate Housing as a Component of the Right to an Adequate Standard of Living, Miloon Kothari, UN Doc. E/CN.4/2005/43, 2005.

12 L. Farha, Report of the Special Rapporteur on Adequate Housing as a Component of the Right to an Adequate Standard of Living, and on the Right to Non-discrimination in this Context, UN Doc. A/71/310, 2016.

13 ECtHR 9 June 2009, no. 33401/02 (Opuz v. Turkey), p. 132.

14 ECtHR 24 April 2012, no. 57693/10 (Kalucza v. Hungary).

15 Commissioner for Human Rights, Recommendation of the Commissioner for Human Rights on the Implementation of the Right to Housing, Strasbourg, Council of Europe, 2009.

At a European level, many countries have laws enabling the eviction of perpetrators of domestic violence while allowing the victim to stay on the property. Proceedings are generally initiated when the police are notified of violent behaviour (Austria, Belgium, Czech Republic, Estonia, Ireland, Italy, Hungary, Latvia, Malta, Slovenia and the United Kingdom).[16] Furthermore, the Council of the European Union has signed the Istanbul Convention on preventing and combating violence against women and domestic violence. As of December 2022, it has been signed by all EU Member States and ratified by 21.[17] However, concerning shelter accommodation accessible to women in the EU after the loss of their home, most fall short of Istanbul Convention requirements. Data collected from EU Member States showcase that 51% of needed beds are currently missing. In European countries outside the EU, 79% of beds are missing. Overall, these figures demonstrate that within Europe, only five countries meet the Istanbul Convention requirements for shelter provision (Liechtenstein, Luxembourg, Malta, Norway, and Slovenia).[18] Considering that the Convention is a relatively new instrument and domestic violence is one of the causes of homelessness, the Convention can nevertheless become a valuable tool to guide policies of the European Union and the Member States, as well as other European countries, in the forthcoming years.

4 Conclusion

In the broader framework, women are vulnerable to homelessness as a result of discriminatory, customary, religious, and statutory laws on divorce, inheritance, and matrimonial property, as well as poor enforcement of recognised basic rights.[19] Thus, whilst it is necessary to acknowledge domestic violence and gender-based violence as a fundamental cause of women's homelessness, it is identically pivotal to examine it in the broader framework of societal problems crisscrossing with socioeconomic and structural hurdles, such as inequalities, poverty, and the lack of affordable housing. What remains clear is that gender dimensions of housing, property, and land as human rights issues, as well as women's equal rights to access, use, and control over land are

16 The Foundation Abbé Pierre & FEANTSA, Second Overview of Housing Exclusion in Europe, Brussels, FEANTSA, 2017.

17 European Parliament, 'EU Accession to the Council of Europe Convention on Preventing and Combating Violence against Women ('Istanbul Convention')', European Parliament, 20 June 2023, https://www.europarl.europa.eu/legislative-train/theme-women-s-rights-and-gender-equality-femm/file-eu-accession-to-the-istanbul-convention?sid=7101 (last accessed 31 July 2023).

18 Women against Violence Europe, WAVE Country Report 2019: The Situation of Women's Specialist Support Services in Europe, Vienna, WAVE – Women against Violence Europe, 2019.

19 UN Committee on the Elimination of Discrimination against Women, General Recommendation on Article 16 of the Convention on the Elimination of All Forms of Discrimination against Women, 26 February 2013, CEDAW/C/GC/29.

additional areas where more work should be done. The development of tools that fully integrate the gender perspective, such as eviction impact assessments or methods for monitoring security of tenure,[20] can help address the specific impact of the loss of one's home situations on women more effectively.

20 OHCHR, Women and the Right to Adequate Housing, Geneva, OHCHR, 2012.

The Efficiency of National Housing Rights: An Overview of France's DALO Law

Andrei-Fabian Balan

1 Introduction

Along the course of the formation of international human rights law, housing has been a historically underrepresented area that has only been highlighted in recent years. The most notable contributions to the expansion of housing rights are their inclusion in the Universal Declaration on Human Rights and International Covenant on Economic, Social and Cultural Rights of the United Nations. Nevertheless, the implementation differs in each state, and data suggests that the UN Committee on Economic, Social and Cultural Rights have so far only examined cases from Spain, most of which were discontinued or deemed inadmissible. This highlights the fact that the implementation and application of international treaties is not uniform in all UN Member States. Regardless, domestic laws have greater chances of achieving tangible results through regulatory bodies and enforcement mechanisms. As such, this paper shall focus on national legislation on the right to housing.

While the responsibility to provide housing to vulnerable individuals or protect them from eviction falls upon each state, many European states that provide a right to housing do not offer a mechanism to implement it.[1] Notwithstanding such a state of affairs, France is an example of a state that has ensured appropriate housing for its inhabitants. This is illustrated by the law 'Droit au Logement Opposable' (DALO),[2] which literally translates to 'Enforceable Right to Housing'. The DALO law was unanimously adopted by the National Assembly of France on 5 March 2007. This law allows individual persons to enforce their right to housing against the state if they live in substandard conditions or if they are disadvantaged in such a way that they are unable to afford adequate housing. This paper aims to provide an accurate assessment of DALO's effectiveness as a right to housing by first offering a brief explanation of its

1 N. Houard & C. Lévy-Vroelant, 'The (Enforceable) Right to Housing: A Paradoxical French Passion', International Journal of Housing Policy, Vol. 13, No. 2, 2013, p. 202.

2 Ibid., pp. 202-203.

enforcement mechanisms, followed by an analysis of the law's implementation and its effects, which will be illustrated through the *Tchokontio Happi v. France* case of the European Court of Human Rights.

2 DALO Enforcement Mechanisms

The DALO entails two types of appeals that are afforded to citizens as well as non-citizens who have a permanent right to residence within France.[3] The first type concerns the prioritisation of people in need of housing by Mediation Committees, which then advise the prefect (the State's representative in a department or region in France) of the people who have been granted priority status regarding housing. A person with priority status is someone who must be housed or re-housed within three to six months or offered temporary accommodation within six weeks.

The second type of appeal deals with people who have not been re-housed by the competent authority within the time period prescribed by law, although they were granted priority status. As a result, a person in this predicament can file an application with the local administrative court to force the prefect to provide them with housing. The state will be fined if the prefect fails to comply. This fine is distributed to a regional fund for social housing. Thus, through the DALO, France has provided its vulnerable inhabitants with the possibility to compel public officials to act in case they fail to uphold their duties regarding social housing. Nonetheless, the prefect's authority remains somewhat limited, as the primary enforcement powers – such as the ability to issue building permits, confer priority status, and decide housing allocations – remain with local authorities.

3 Effectiveness of DALO

The DALO law's overall effectiveness in protecting vulnerable individuals by providing them with adequate housing has been called into question multiple times since the law was adopted. The law has undoubtedly contributed to positive effects within the social housing sector by helping to re-house many vulnerable individuals, and the fact that the right to housing has been made enforceable is a noteworthy development, thereby fundamentally solidifying the importance of housing. However, according to the available

3 C. Mialot & J. Ponce, 'Ten Years of the French DALO and the Catalan Right to Housing Act: European Innovation in the Fields of Land Use Planning and Housing', Journal of Comparative Urban Law and Policy, Vol. 2, No. 1, 2017, pp. 101-128.

data, 950,000 appeals have been filed since the law came into force, among which only 270,000 have been granted priority status, and only 167,200 have been re-housed.[4] Therefore, a significant number of individuals with priority status have not received the necessary housing allotted to them based on the DALO law.

In recent years, a growing housing crisis has been observed, particularly in the Île-de-France region, which includes the populous French capital of Paris. Despite the fact that there has been a growing number of homeless persons (from 2001 to 2012, homelessness increased by 58%), there has been a decrease in the number of persons being granted priority status. This was mentioned by the High Committee for Housing of Disadvantaged Persons, which called attention to the fact that Mediation Committees were not in compliance with the law.[5] The High Committee observed that the Mediation Committees were increasingly using informal criteria to decide individual cases (such as taking into account housing availability), as opposed to only utilising the criteria laid down in the law proper (by focusing primarily on the situation of the vulnerable person in question). The system itself suffers from the disparity between supply and demand of social housing as well as from procedural inconsistency: each local Mediation Committee differs significantly in its methods on how to decide who receives priority status. Factors that also influence the situation are the lack of resources required to functionally process the hundreds of applications received by the Mediation Committees and the lack of necessary data on the measure to accurately assess the need for housing.

4 *Tchokontio Happi v. France* (2015)

A particularly poignant example of the issues that have arisen in implementing the DALO law is the *Tchokontio Happi v. France* case that was adjudicated by the European Court of Human Rights (ECtHR) in 2015.[6] The case concerns Elizabeth Tchokontio Happi (hereafter referred to as 'the applicant'), a citizen of Cameroon who has lived in France since 2003 and was granted priority status by the Paris Mediation Committee in 2010 on the basis of the DALO law. Unfortunately, the applicant had not been re-housed six months after being granted priority status in accordance with the DALO law, and she

---

4 OHCHR, 'End of Mission Statement by The Special Rapporteur on the Right to Adequate Housing Presents Her Preliminary Findings after Her Visit to the Republic of France, Conducted on 2-11 April, 2019', OHCHR, 12 April 2019, https://www.ohchr.org/en/statements/2019/04/end-mission-statement-special-rapporteur-right-adequate-housing-presents-her?LangID=E&NewsID=24475 (last accessed 1 August 2023).

5 M.A. Carlotti, L'effectivité du droit au logement opposable: Mission d'évaluation dans 14 départements, Paris, Haut Comité pour le Logement des Personnes Défavorisées, 2016.

6 ECtHR 9 April 2015, no. 65829/12 (Tchokontio v. France).

filed an application with the Paris Administrative Court. The application was upheld, and the Paris Administrative Court ordered the prefect to re-house the applicant, imposing a €700 monthly fine on the French State until the matter was concluded. Nevertheless, the applicant had still not been re-housed two years later and, therefore, filed an application with the ECtHR under Article 6(1) of the European Convention on Human Rights (ECHR), the right to a fair trial. The applicant also filed a complaint under Article 1 of Protocol No. 1 to the ECHR concerning property protection.

The ECtHR found that the applicant had not been re-housed within the six-month period required by the DALO law, even though the applicant was granted priority status. The French Government argued that the fine imposed by the authorities was in accordance with the aim of the law to ensure compliance from state authorities, highlighting the coercive nature of the fine. The ECtHR rejected the argument, concluding that the fine imposed on the authorities by the Paris Administrative Court went to a state fund for social housing, which was not paid to the applicant herself. As such, the fine had no compensatory function and had essentially no effect in obligating the state authorities to re-house the applicant, a fact that was emphasised by the Government's failure to find housing for the applicant even after three- and-a-half years. The French Government tried to argue that a lack of resources and funds excused its failure to uphold its responsibilities. Yet, the ECtHR found the argument unpersuasive and argued that authorities could not excuse their failure to take the necessary measures because of a lack of financial assets on their part.

The ECtHR decided that the failure of the French authorities to enforce the judgement of the Paris Administrative Court for several years deprived Article 6(1) ECHR of all useful effect and, consequently, found that France had violated the applicant's rights. On the other hand, the ECtHR deemed inadmissible the applicant's claim under Article 1 of Protocol No. 1 ECHR that the actions of the authorities constituted a violation of the protection of property, as the applicant's right to social housing would not be considered possession within the meaning of the respective Article.

The ECtHR's decision highlights the core problems in the implementation of the DALO law. The lack of resources for the enforcement of this law, along with the authorities' negligence to take the measures required to end the unfortunate situation that Ms Tchokontio Happi was confronted with, underline the reduced effectiveness of the law and the dire situation in which a considerable number of vulnerable people are left.

5 Conclusion

The DALO law is necessary in order to improve the lives of many vulnerable citizens, and it is inarguably a step forward for housing rights as a whole. However, the implementation of the law reveals a significant number of issues, such as fragmented application, competing social goals and a lack of adequate housing. In order to ensure greater efficiency, the law must be strongly monitored and supported by the government as well as NGOs, citizens, and other relevant actors. If the competent authorities (the prefects) are unable to maintain collaborative relationships with social housing providers and local authorities, the system risks failure in achieving its intended goals, thereby casting a shadow on its credibility and effectiveness. As such, the DALO law has aided a lot of vulnerable persons, but it has the potential to assist many more if the authorities can overcome the underlying challenges that hinder its effectiveness.

Criminalising Homelessness: The Case of Area Bans in the Netherlands

Els Schipaanboord and Michel Vols

1 Introduction

Homelessness remains a significant societal issue throughout Europe. The *Eighth Overview of Housing Exclusion in Europe*, published in 2023 by FEANTSA and the Abbé Pierre Foundation, revealed that approximately 895,000 individuals are homeless in Europe.[1] This staggering number demonstrates that even one of the wealthiest continents worldwide struggles to effectively implement some fundamental aspects of the right to adequate housing, as outlined in Article 11 of the ICESCR and Article 31 of the Revised European Social Charter.[2]

Recent research has been conducted on homelessness and the right to adequate housing. One area of focus has been the analysis of Housing First programmes, assessed through the lens of the right to adequate housing.[3] Another area of research has evaluated how eviction protections are implemented in national jurisdictions to prevent homelessness.[4]

This paper aims to contribute to research on the criminalisation of homelessness and the right to adequate housing. The concept of criminalisation of homelessness refers to

---

1 Report: 8th Overview of Housing Exclusion in Europe 2023, https://www.feantsa.org/en/report/2023/09/05/report-8th-overview-of-housing-exclusion-in-europe-2023, pp. 15-24.

2 E. Sweeney, L.M. Bruijn & M. Vols, 'Deconstructing the Eviction Protections under the Revised European Social Charter: A Systematic Content Analysis of the Interplay between the Right to Housing and the Right to Property', Human Rights Law Review, Vol. 23, No. 4, 2023, pp. 1-25.

3 S.L. Stadler & D. Collins, 'Assessing Housing First Programs from a Right to Housing Perspective', Housing Studies, Vol. 38, No. 9, 2023, pp. 1719-1739.

4 L.M. Bruijn, The Alternative War on Drugs: Drug Evictions, Cannabis Regulation and the Legal Consequences of Adapting to the Limitations of Criminal Law in the Field of Drug Control, Groningen, University of Groningen, 2021; M. Vols, 'The Optional Protocol to the ICESCR, Homelessness and Moral Hazard: The Alternative Adequate Housing Requirement in the CESCR's Jurisprudence – An Incentive Not to Pay for Housing?', International Human Rights Law Review, Vol. 12, No. 1, 2023, pp. 1-25.

> formal and informal measures and enforcement policies to limit where individuals who experience homelessness can congregate, and punish those who engage in life-sustaining or natural human activities in public spaces.[5]

An example of criminalising homelessness is making it illegal to sleep, sit, or store personal belongings in public spaces.[6] Regulations prohibiting begging or removing items from rubbish bins can also be characterised as criminalising homelessness.[7]

In this paper, we examine area bans (or exclusion orders) as an instrument that may criminalise homelessness. Area bans are orders issued by (local) authorities to individuals to bar them from entering or staying in certain geographical areas. These areas may be more or less specifically designated streets, squares, public buildings, or other infrastructure such as train stations, neighbourhoods, or even larger parts of a city. In some countries, area bans may be issued by a court in criminal proceedings, but in other countries, area bans are issued by administrative authorities such as the mayor. Non-compliance with area bans typically results in criminal offences and hefty fines or imprisonment for violators. Area bans are used in various countries worldwide and have been studied widely.[8] In this paper, however, we evaluate the usage of area bans in the Netherlands, specifically targeting homeless individuals.

2 Area Bans in the Netherlands

The mayors in the Netherlands have the authority to impose area bans under different pieces of legislation. The Municipality Act of 1992 gives mayors the power to issue an area ban in case of a serious disturbance of public order.[9] Additionally, local ordinances give mayors similar authority. The municipality of Rotterdam, for example, has a bylaw

5 S. Jones (Ed.), Mean Streets. A Report on the Criminalisation of Homelessness in Europe, Brussels, FEANTSA, 2013, p. 15.

6 See M. Killander, 'Criminalising Homelessness and Survival Strategies through Municipal By-Laws: Colonial Legacy and Constitutionality', South African Journal on Human Rights, Vol. 35, No. 1, 2019, pp. 70-93; L. Faragó et al., 'Criminalization as a Justification for Violence against the Homeless in Hungary', The Journal of Social Psychology, Vol. 162, No. 2, 2022, pp. 216-230.

7 See D.J. Baker, 'A Critical Evaluation of the Historical and Contemporary Justifications for Criminalising Begging Comment', Journal of Criminal Law, Vol. 73, No. 3, 2009, pp. 212-240; S.Y. Rahman, 'The Beggar as a Political Symbol: An Interactionist Reading of the Endurance of Anti-Begging Laws in India', Social Change, Vol. 51, No. 2, 2021, pp. 206-225; N. Lgarah & L. MacLean, 'Bedelverboden: van ordeprobleem tot mensenrechtenkwestie', Ars Aequi, Vol. 6, 2021, p. 523.

8 See, for example, B. Belina, 'From Disciplining To Dislocation: Area Bans in Recent Urban Policing in Germany', European Urban and Regional Studies, Vol. 14, No. 4, 2007, pp. 321-236; K. Beckett & S. Herbert, Banished: The New Social Control in Urban America, Oxford, Oxford University Press, 2012.

9 Arts. 172(3) and 172a Gemeentewet 1992.

that allows the mayor to issue an area ban to individuals who disturb public order or commit criminal offences. This is done to ensure public safety, prevent or limit nuisance, protect the living environment, ensure the safety of people and property, and uphold health and morality standards.[10]

Research shows area bans are used to fight various types of disorder, including football hooliganism and religious extremism.[11] Yet, it is clear that the area bans target homeless people as well.[12] This becomes evident, too, if we analyse some recent case law on area bans.

3 DUTCH CASE LAW ON AREA BANS

Five recent Dutch court rulings have highlighted the significant impact of an imposed area ban.[13] In each of these cases, the individuals who were sanctioned were homeless. They claimed to rely on the designated area for which the area ban was imposed. They also suffered from substance abuse. In three of these cases, the case dealt with the legality of the area ban itself. In these cases, the judge ruled in favour of the mayor, stipulating that the judge hoped that the area ban would lead to accepting help.[14] Criminal court delivered the other two judgements. In the Netherlands, violating a mayor-imposed area ban is considered a felony and can lead to criminal prosecution. In the two criminal cases the homeless individuals were sentenced to two years for treatment of their addiction.[15] These two final cases demonstrate the potential consequences of area bans and the severity of the associated criminal sanctions for violating them.

---

10 Art. 2:77b APV Rotterdam 2023, http://lokaleregelgeving.overheid.nl/CVDR373493/18.

11 M. van Rooij et al., 'Bestrijding van voetbalgeweld', Ars Aequi, Vol. 11, 2016, pp. 809-819; J.G. Brouwer & A.E. Schilder, 'Het gebiedsverbod als wapen tegen verspreiding van jihadistisch gedachtegoed', Justitiële verkenningen, Vol. 44, No. 2, 2018, pp. 58-69.

12 A. Sibma et al., Op Doel?, The Hague, WODC, 2012, p. 65; M.I. Tuk & L.M. van den Bor, 'De toepassing van gebiedsverboden op grond van de gewijzigde Wet MBVEO in de praktijk', De Gemeentestem, Vol. 7493, 2019, p. 578; H. Winter et al., Evaluatie Wet maatregelen bestrijding voetbalvandalisme en ernstige overlast, The Hague, WODC, 2021.

13 District Court The Hague 20 July 2022, ECLI:NL:RBDHA:2022:9198; District Court The Hague 20 July 2022, ECLI:NL:RBDHA:2022:9201; District Court The Hague 20 July 2022, ECLI:NL:RBDHA:2022:9200; District Court Amsterdam 26 April 2023, ECLI:NL:RBAMS:2023:3532; District Court The Hague 9 November 2023, ECLI:NL:RBDHA:2023:17139.

14 District Court The Hague 20 July 2022, ECLI:NL:RBDHA:2022:9198; District Court The Hague 20 July 2022, ECLI:NL:RBDHA:2022:9201; District Court The Hague 20 July 2022, ECLI:NL:RBDHA:2022:9200.

15 District Court Amsterdam 26 April 2023, ECLI:NL:RBAMS:2023:3532; District Court The Hague 9 November 2023, ECLI:NL:RBDHA:2023:17139.

4 Area Bans and European Human Rights

It is noteworthy that the right to adequate housing is not mentioned in cases on area bans and homelessness available in the Dutch online case law database. This might be surprising because it is a common belief that homelessness should be recognised as an extreme violation of this right.[16] Yet, in reality, the right often only offers assistance (if any) to those already housed. Housing outsiders, such as people experiencing homelessness, do not have such a stable (legal) foundation from which to start.[17]

This, however, does not mean that human rights do not play a role in the context of area bans at all. Of course, area bans limit someone's right to liberty of movement as laid down in, *inter alia*, Article 2 of the Fourth Protocol to the ECHR. When it comes to homeless individuals, one could argue that imposing an area ban restricts their right to freedom to choose their residence, as stated in the same Article. After all, the streets, porches, benches, and bridges – the very places from which they are banned – could be considered their potential places of residence. Even though the Netherlands has ratified the Fourth Protocol to the ECHR and accepted the rights of liberty of movement and freedom to choose one's residence, the published case law does not indicate that Dutch courts frequently recognise and uphold these rights in cases on area bans imposed on homeless individuals. Two relatively old cases, not dealing with a homeless person, ended up with the European Court of European Rights (ECtHR). In *Landvreugd v. The Netherlands* and *Oliveira v. the Netherlands*, the ECtHR ruled that the mayor of Amsterdam had legitimately limited the right to liberty of movement because all the criteria in the limitation clauses had been met.[18]

Of course, it should not be assumed that all claims based on Article 2 of the Fourth Protocol, in the context of area bans imposed on homeless individuals, lack merit. One may argue that in specific contexts, issuing an area ban is not justified in the public interest in a democratic society (para. 4 of Art. 2) or necessary in a democratic society (para. 3 of Art. 2). This argument primarily concerns the proportionality of the area ban. The argument's success greatly depends on the context of the case in which it is presented. Having decent legal representation and procedural safeguards will surely increase the likelihood of successfully challenging an area ban.

---

16 UN Human Rights Council (HRC), Report of the Special Rapporteur on Adequate Housing as a Component of the Right to an Adequate Standard of Living, and on the Right to Non-discrimination in This Context, 30 December 2015, A/HRC/31/54, via https://digitallibrary.un.org/record/831237, p. 3.

17 See M. Pieterse, 'Towards a Right to the City?: The Slow Convergence of Rights to Housing and Land in South African Constitutional Jurisprudence', International Human Rights Law Review, Vol. 11, No. 1, 2022, p. 54.

18 ECtHR 4 June 2002, no. 37331/97 (Landvreugd v. The Netherlands); ECtHR 4 June 2002, no. 33129/96 (Olivieira v. The Netherlands).

One may think Article 6 of the ECHR provides procedural protection to homeless individuals facing an area ban. Yet, under Dutch law, issuing an area ban is not characterised as charging someone with a criminal offence. In the legal realm, area bans are seen as an administrative sanction, purely reparatory and not punitive in nature. Research indicates, however, that in real life, area bans and other reparatory administrative sanctions are experienced as punitive by both the sanctioned persons and governmental officers involved in imposing the sanctions.[19] Nevertheless, the hegemonic nature of the legal qualification of area bans implies that important safeguards, such as the right to have adequate time and facilities to prepare a defence, enshrined in Article 6 of the ECHR are lacking.[20] This also holds for, for example, the right to have the free assistance of an interpreter if one cannot understand or speak the language used in court.

5 CONCLUSION

The lack of a right to have the free assistance of an interpreter is especially relevant in the context of area bans imposed on homeless individuals. Statistical data collected by Statistics Netherlands (CBS) shows that in 2022, almost 40% of homeless individuals in the Netherlands were born in another European country (5%) or outside Europe (35%). Another 21% of homeless individuals in the Netherlands were born in the Netherlands but have parents born outside Europe. This suggests that a significant proportion of homeless people in the Netherlands may not speak Dutch or at least struggle to understand it.[21] This finding challenges the notion that homeless people are adequately protected against area bans, exposing disparities between government expectations and citizens' capabilities.[22]

Besides that, one may argue that imposing an area ban on a homeless individual is a setup for failure anyway. Of course, we must consider that temporarily removing individuals who cause public disorder may relieve affected communities. Imposing an

19 See R. Salet & H. Sackers, 'Spanningen tussen de bestuurlijke en strafrechtelijke aanpak van criminaliteit', Nederlands Juristenblad, Vol. 14, 2019, p. 937. See also Beckett & Herbert, 2012, p. 104.

20 See M. Vols & D. Duran, 'Tackling Anti-Social Behaviour and Homelessness with Exclusion Orders in the Netherlands, Belgium, England and Wales', in G.J. Vonk & A. Tollenaar (Eds.), Homelessness and the Law, Oisterwijk, Wolf Legal Publishers, 2014, pp. 61-72.

21 See https://www.cbs.nl/nl-nl/nieuws/2023/39/26-6-duizend-dakloze-mensen-begin-2022 (last accessed 2 December 2023). See also M. Rooij, 'Verbanning uit het semipublieke domein', Justitiële verkenningen, Vol. 44, No. 2, 2018, p. 20.

22 See Wetenschappelijke Raad voor het Regeringsbeleid (WRR), 'Weten is nog geen doen. Een realistisch perspectief op redzaamheid', 2017, https://www.wrr.nl/publicaties/rapporten/2017/04/24/weten-is-nog-geen-doen (last accessed 2 December 2023).

area ban on a highly dependent individual unlikely to comply is ineffective. It should result in serious doubts on the proportionality of the area ban in court. Research on area bans showed that professionals involved in imposing these bans recognised this setup for failure in the context of homeless individuals.[23] In cases where homelessness leads to disturbances and disorder, a human-rights-based approach would suggest providing care and housing support instead of further marginalising homeless individuals. They are already victims of human rights violations, and criminalisation would only add to their suffering.

23 Winter, 2021, pp. 52-54 & 75.

Part II
Occupancy Rights

Introduction to Occupancy Rights

Michelle Bruijn and Stefan van Tongeren

The timeless maxim, "For a man's house is his castle, *et domus sua cuique tutissimum refugium* [and his home his safest refuge]",[1] encapsulates the essence of the castle doctrine, a concept historically rooted in the right of individuals to safeguard their homes against external threats. Originally, this doctrine granted individuals the right to use force, even lethal force, to protect their home, providing a legal shield against prosecution in case of harm to an intruder. Over time, however, the meaning has evolved to symbolise the home as a personal sanctuary – a place where one should feel safe and secure, shielded from external forces.[2]

In the contemporary context, the castle doctrine extends beyond mere physical protection, embodying the broader notions of privacy, autonomy, and control within the confines of one's home. It serves as a foundational principle supporting the right to quiet enjoyment and providing legal safeguards against unreasonable search and seizure. These protections are considered vital for upholding personal freedom and autonomy in a society that values individual privacy.[3]

Within the framework of the right to housing, the first paper of this book ('Conceptualising the Right to Housing') classifies these elements as occupancy rights. This part of the book delves into various manifestations of occupancy rights, shedding light on the right to privacy and the significance of being undisturbed in one's home. It explores the concept of habitability, emphasising the need for protection against environmental influences and natural disasters, and ensuring adequate living conditions for individuals with disabilities. Moreover, the papers underscore the intricate connections between occupancy rights and other fundamental human rights. Authors delve into the intersections with the right to privacy, the right to life, and the right to health, emphasising the symbiotic relationship between occupancy rights and the overall well-being of individuals. Central to this exploration are the state obligations to ensure and protect fundamental rights associated with occupancy.

---

1 E. Coke, Third Part of the Institutes of the Laws of England: Concerning High Treason, and Other Pleas of the Crown, and Criminal Causes, Bell-Yard, E. and R. Brooke, 1797, p. 161.

2 D.M. Drake, 'The Castle Doctrine: An Expanding Right to Stand Your Ground', St. Mary's Law Journal, Vol. 39, No. 3, 2007, p. 573-613.

3 G.S. Dickinson, 'The Fourth Amendment's Constitutional Home', William & Mary Bill of Rights Journal, Vol. 31, No. 4, 2023, pp. 1063-1134; L.C. McClain, 'Inviolability and Privacy: The Castle, the Sanctuary, and the Body', Yale Journal of Law & Humanities, Vol. 7, 1995, pp. 195-241; M. Walzer, 'Liberalism and the Art of Separation', Political Theory, Vol. 12, No. 3, 1984, p. 317.

As we navigate through the following papers, it becomes evident that occupancy rights is not an isolated concept but an integral component of a broader framework that seeks to guarantee individuals a dignified, secure, and healthy living environment.

Loss of a Home and the Inevitable Loss of a Private Life: A Case for More Privacy-Friendly Shelters

Maria Niemelä

1 Introduction: The Dimensions of the Right to Private Life

The right to respect for private life under Article 8 of the European Convention on Human Rights (ECHR) entails the right to be left alone in our privacy. Having privacy serves as the foundation for living our private lives, free from unwarranted State interference. The origins of the right to privacy are linked to property,[1] but the right has evolved beyond the physical plane since then to include mental integrity, reputation, and social life of a person.[2] However, the importance of spatial privacy should not be underestimated, which is evidenced by the fact that the exercise of a plethora of other rights is tied to having a home.

A large part of our private lives is lived at home. The home provides shelter from storms and ensures a secure environment to cultivate our thoughts and beliefs. Thus, having adequate privacy establishes a foundation for personal growth and the establishment of meaningful connections with others. Undoubtedly, the home plays a pivotal role in shaping the human experience, and it is crucial that this enjoyment is not denied to those who find themselves homeless.

2 The Right to Privacy and the Right to Housing

The loss of a home marks an instance where both the right to live our private lives and the right to housing are engaged. The loss of a home is a prima facie violation of the right

1 S. DaCosta, 'Privacy-as-Property: A New Fundamental Approach to the Right to Privacy and the Impact This Will Have on the Law and Corporations', CMC Senior Theses, 2021.

2 European Court of Human Rights, Guide on Article 8 of the Convention – Right to respect for private and family life, Strasbourg, European Court of Human Rights, 2022.

to adequate housing,[3] which State parties to the International Covenant on Economic, Social and Cultural Rights (ICESCR) are obligated to progressively realise to the fullest extent of their available resources. The right is thus a second-generation right, existing to pursue the attainment of social justice. *Au contraire*, the right to privacy, enshrined in Article 17 of the International Convention on Civil and Political Rights (ICCPR), is generally understood to exist to limit state power. However, the right to privacy may also trigger positive obligations on the part of the State to ensure that individual rights are respected.

3 The Loss of a Home and Alternative Housing under the Right to Privacy and the Right to Housing

It should be borne in mind that the enforcement of second-generation rights is subject to much more debate compared to the enforcement of first-generation rights. Therefore, it may be more effective for individuals who have lost their home to enforce their rights under the right to privacy, compared to the right to housing.

In the case *Liliana Assenova Naibidenova et al. v. Bulgaria*, it was held by the Human Rights Committee that evictions resulting in homelessness violate a person's right to privacy when no satisfactory alternative housing is immediately available.[4] While the right to private life under Article 8 ECHR cannot be interpreted as the right to be provided with a home,[5] it is important given the link between the privacy enabled by a home and the enjoyment of one's family and social life, that privacy considerations are included in the criteria for what constitutes satisfactory alternative housing.

4 The Current State of Affairs

In the current state of affairs, many shelters for those experiencing homelessness do not provide adequate privacy. This absence of privacy has far-reaching consequences on their physical and mental well-being. For instance, dormitory-style accommodation often features a common room with multiple beds in an open space. Many fear for their

3 UN Human Rights Council (HRC), Guidelines for the Implementation of the Right to Adequate Housing: Report of the Special Rapporteur on Adequate Housing as a Component of the Right to an Adequate Standard of Living, and on the Right to Non-discrimination in this Context, 26 December 2019, A/HRC/43/43, p. 7.

4 Human Rights Committee, Liliana Assenova Naibidenova et al. v. Bulgaria: Communication No. 2073/2011, UN Doc. CCPR/C/106/D/2073/2011, 27 November 2012.

5 ECtHR 18 January 2001, no. 27238/95 (Chapman v. The United Kingdom).

personal integrity, as well as the safety of their possessions.[6] For some, the lack of privacy is a reason not to go to a shelter. Other alternatives that individuals may resort to include seeking temporary accommodation with relatives or friends, one's car, a tent, or even living on the streets.[7] Staying in a shelter should be a temporary relief in the process of finding affordable housing with tenure security, and it is a stepping stone to securing the right to adequate housing. However, for the sake of preserving human dignity of those experiencing homelessness, it is crucial that their enjoyment of the rights derived from their right to privacy continue in the shelter to the maximum extent possible.

5 Conclusion

Suggestions for action include having adequate space in shelters to dedicate rooms for socialising and family time, which form a vital part of a person's private life, as well as securing spatial privacy in the form of having locked lockers for one's possessions and curtains around one's bed. What constitutes adequate housing, such as cultural adequacy and having adequate space for studying, may also impact a person's enjoyment of the person's private life.

By implementing these measures, we can strive to ensure that individuals experiencing homelessness are afforded the opportunity to maintain their human dignity and enjoy their rights derived from the right to privacy, even within the confines of a temporary shelter, to the greatest extent possible. It is evident that the right to housing and the right to privacy are interdependent in this regard.

6 M.R. Taylor & E.T. Walsh, 'When Corporal Acts Are Labeled Criminal: Lack of Privacy among the Homeless', Sociology Mind, Vol. 8, No. 2, 2018, pp. 130-142.

7 European Commission, 'Employment, Social Affairs & Inclusion', European Commission, https://ec.europa.eu/social/main.jsp?catId=1061&langId=en (last accessed 3 August 2023).

Constructing Peace, Security, and Dignity: One Building Permit at a Time – The Obligation to Monitor the Habitability of Housing at the Heart of Preventing Damages Caused by Natural Disasters

Maria Niemelä

1 Introduction

Ensuring that housing is built in a safe manner is integral to the right to adequate housing. In other words, a place of residence cannot be considered adequate if it does not guarantee the physical safety of the occupant.[1] The requirement of habitability of housing is where the rights to housing, life, and property coincide.[2]

This link recently proved evident when the violent earthquakes rattled Turkey and Syria in February 2023. The event led to the destruction of 160,000 buildings[3] in only Turkey and, consequently, a severe loss of life. The scale of the humanitarian crisis has been attributed to the poor quality of housing in the country,[4] raising questions as to the responsibility of the State under international human rights law when it comes to the prevention and mitigation of damage that results from a natural disaster.

1 UN Office of the High Commissioner for Human Rights (OHCHR), Fact Sheet No. 21 (Rev. 1): The Human Right to Adequate Housing, 2009, p. 4.

2 K. Istrefi, 'Earthquakes in Türkiye and the Right to Life: Whither Positive Obligations?', ECHR Blog, 13 February 2023, https://www.echrblog.com/2023/02/earthquakes-in-turkiye-and-right-to.html (last accessed 4 August 2023).

3 E. Toksabay & O. Coskun, 'Turkey Begins to Rebuild for 1.5 million Left Homeless by Earthquakes', Reuters, 25 February 2023, https://www.reuters.com/world/middle-east/turkey-issues-earthquake-rebuilding-rules-after-millions-left-homeless-2023-02-24/ (last accessed 4 August 2023).

4 A. Thompson, 'Why the Earthquake in Turkey Was So Damaging and Deadly', Scientific American, 6 February 2023, https://www.scientificamerican.com/article/why-the-earthquake-in-turkey-was-so-damaging-and-deadly/ (last accessed 8 August 2023).

2 Protection of Life in the Context of Natural Disasters

The responsibility of states in connection to natural disasters is tricky terrain, given their lack of control over such events. The European Court of Human Rights (hereinafter: the ECtHR) looked at the issue through the lens of the right to life (Art. 2 of the European Convention on Human Rights) in the case of *Budayeva and others v. Russia*.[5] The ECtHR noted that the obligation towards citizens to protect their right to life applies "in the context of any activity … in which the right to life may be at stake",[6] including situations in which the right to life is threatened by a natural disaster.[7] The criteria for establishing the extent of the State's positive obligations when it comes to protecting its citizens from natural disasters can be found in para. 137 of the same judgement. According to the ECtHR, it is important to consider the origin of the threat and its imminence, considering the area's susceptibility to such threats. Following the ECtHR's reasoning, being situated in a highly seismologically active region increases the positive obligations of the state to take action to protect its citizens from harm.

In the context of ensuring habitable housing, the protection comes mostly in the form of preventive measures to mitigate future damage. In this regard, the ECtHR noted the position of the state at the frontline of risk prevention in the case of *Özel and others v. Turkey*.[8] Namely, ensuring appropriate spatial planning and a controlled urban environment by way of regulation were denoted as important factors in mitigating damage arising from natural disasters.

What was found in the current case is that the State had fulfilled its duty to set appropriate standards. Namely, following the Izmit earthquake in 1999, a more stringent building code was adopted to build earthquake-proof housing and ensure that houses were structurally adequate to protect their occupants.[9] Moreover, the state devised a national housing policy in 2018 to target the housing built prior to the

---

5 ECtHR 20 March 2008, nos. 15339/02, 21166/02, 20058/02, 11673/02 and 15343/02 (Budayeva and others v. Russia).

6 ECtHR 20 March 2008, Budayeva and others v. Russia, p. 130.

7 Ibid., pp. 135, 137.

8 ECtHR 17 November 2015, nos. 14350/05, 15245/05 and 16051/05 (Özel and others v. Turkey), pp. 170-174.

9 P. Beaumont, 'Turkey Earthquake Death Toll Prompts Questions over Building Standards', The Guardian, 7 February 2023, https://www.theguardian.com/global-development/2023/feb/07/turkey-earthquakes-death-toll-prompts-questions-over-building-standards (last accessed 4 August 2023).

adoption of the new code and attempt large-scale renovations to ensure the inhabitants' right to housing, life, and property.[10]

3 The 2023 Turkey–Syria Earthquake

Crucial to the success of regulation and policies is the implementation that is secured by way of monitoring and enforcement, which was seemingly lacking in Turkey. The earthquakes exposed severe structural weaknesses, even in the newly built houses, despite the existence of building standards.[11] The root of the issue was found to be the practice of 'construction amnesties' issued by the government, under which, pursuant to payment, it is possible to get a building permit regardless of the building standards in place.[12] Such has been the practice since the 1960s, leading to the adoption of hundreds of thousands of building permits devoid of meaning and, with that, misconceptions as to the safety of the homes in question.[13] In 2020 alone, 672,000 buildings were granted the amnesty.[14] The practice of construction amnesties fails to ensure a controlled urban environment – something that the ECtHR noted to be an important factor in mitigating the damages of natural disasters and, consequently, complying with the positive obligations arising from the right to life.

4 Conclusion

It follows that the combination of regulating, monitoring, and enforcing the habitability of housing is essential for preventing significant losses of life during natural disasters. The humanitarian crisis taking place in Turkey exemplifies the devastating scenario that follows when there is no monitoring of compliance with the legislation governing the habitability of housing. The monitoring of compliance is a crucial factor that the State

10 See the questionnaire issued by the UN Special Rapporteur on adequate housing as a component of the right to an adequate standard of living, and on the right to non-discrimination in this context: https://www.ohchr.org/sites/default/files/Documents/Issues/Housing/sub-nationalgovernments/311014_Istanbul_Bilgi_U_TurkeyEN.docx (last accessed 4 August 2023).

11 J. Horton & W. Armstrong, 'Turkey Earthquake: Why Did So Many Buildings Collapse?', BBC, 9 February 2023, https://www.bbc.com/news/64568826 (last accessed 4 August 2023).

12 K. Harrington, 'How Turkey's "Construction Amnesties" Created a Ticking Time Bomb', Jacobin, 6 March 2023, https://jacobin.com/2023/03/turkey-erdogan-construction-amnesty-building-collapse-earthquake-deaths (last accessed 4 August 2023).

13 J. Green, 'Buildings that Should Not Have Collapsed during the Earthquake in Turkey', The Storiest, 9 February 2023, https://thestoriest.com/world/254075.html (last accessed 4 August 2023).

14 Horton & Armstrong, 2023.

can control to mitigate the impact of such disasters, ultimately enabling citizens to live in peace, security, and dignity.[15]

15 L. Farha, Special Rapporteur on the Right to Adequate Housing, The Right to Life & the Right to Housing: Presentation to the Human Rights Committee, 11 July 2016, https://www.ohchr.org/sites/default/files/Documents/Issues/Housing/TB/HousingPresentation.pdf (last accessed 4 August 2023).

Housing Rights as an Avenue to Environmental Protection: The ECtHR Continues Its Efforts in *Solyanik v. Russia*

Lea Schubert

1 Introduction

The European Court of Human Rights (hereinafter: ECtHR) has a long tradition of adjudicating housing issues in the context of several human rights protected in the European Convention of Human Rights (ECHR). Examples of the provisions referred to in this regard include Articles 2, 3, 6, 8, 13, and 14 ECHR. This fragmentation of rights over several different ECHR provisions is also followed in the ECtHR's recent jurisdiction on environmental issues.

Although the right to a clean environment does not exist as such under the ECHR, the ECtHR has ruled on cases involving the environment by making creative use of different ECHR rights, such as those protected in Articles 2, 6, 8, 10, and 13 ECHR.[1] By referring to the same Articles that inspire its jurisprudence on housing rights, the ECtHR has thereby repeatedly combined issues of environmental protection with housing issues. An example of this approach can be observed in the recent case *Solyanik v. Russia*, in which the ECtHR adjudicates pollution in the context of the right to respect for private and family life and the home under Article 8 ECHR.[2]

2 Background of the Case

The case concerned a Russian national, Vladimir Vladislavovich Solyanik, who owns a house and an adjacent area of land in Vladivostok, Russia. The land is located near a cemetery, which was closed in 1995 when its maximum capacity was reached. Despite

1 B. Alan, 'Human Rights and the Environment: Where Next?', European Journal of International Law, Vol. 23, 2012, pp. 613-642.
2 ECtHR 10 May 2022, no. 47987/15 (Solyanik v. Russia).

the closure, burials continued to take place at the cemetery, leading the applicant to start court proceedings to prevent them. At several points before and during the proceedings, the soil of the applicant's land and the water of his well (his only source of drinking water) were tested by forensic experts who found serious abnormalities in their chemical composition, which could be traced back to the proximity of the cemetery. Furthermore, it was established during the domestic court proceedings that a sanitary protection zone should have been established after the cemetery's expansion, as domestic law required. Yet, this never took place. Despite taking note of this fact, the Regional Court refused the applicant's request to put an end to the burials. After unsuccessful appeals before the Regional Court and the Supreme Court, the applicant brought the case before the ECtHR.

3 The Decision of the ECtHR

The applicant complained to the ECtHR on the basis of his right to respect for his private and family life and his home under Article 8 ECHR. He argued that the cemetery was polluting the soil of his land and his only source of drinking water and was therefore negatively affecting his home and his and his family's health. Examining the existence of an interference, the ECtHR restated its previous case law on environmental claims requiring the alleged interference to directly affect the applicant's home or private and family life and to be of a sufficient degree of seriousness.

Although there was no direct detrimental effect on the applicant's health in this case, the ECtHR ruled that the burials negatively affected his home. It relied on the fact that the cemetery had been expanded without establishing a sanitary protection zone and on the forensic reports testifying to the environmental risks posed to his home. The ECtHR, therefore, found an interference under Article 8 ECHR.

The ECtHR then continued to adjudicate on the merits of the case. It found that the authorities′ continuation with the burials was not in compliance with domestic law as it violated both the decree ordering the closure of the cemetery and several health regulations concerning burials. The government's argument that no violation had taken place since enforcement proceedings were pending at the domestic level was dismissed. By finding that the conduct was contrary to domestic law, the ECtHR found it unnecessary to rule on the questions of whether there was a legitimate aim and whether it was necessary in a democratic society. Therefore, the ECtHR concluded that the applicant's rights under Article 8 ECHR had been violated.

4 Continuing the Effort to Combine Environmental Issues and Housing Issues

While the conclusion reached by the ECtHR seems straightforward due to the authorities' failure to comply with national law, it reflects an interesting development in the ECtHR's adjudication of environmental claims. By referring to the negative effect of the pollution on the applicant's home to establish a violation of Article 8 ECHR, the ECtHR effectively combines environmental and housing issues. One interesting aspect in this regard is that the ECtHR found an interference despite no actual damage to the applicant. The ECtHR's willingness to relax the threshold of a 'sufficient degree of seriousness' usually required for an interference under Article 8 ECHR shows its commitment to using housing rights to adjudicate environmental claims.

This trend is in line with the ECtHR's previous case law on environmental issues. In *Solyanik v. Russia*, the ECtHR follows its recent judgment in *Fadeya*, the first environmental case involving Russia, which the ECtHR also dealt with under Article 8 ECHR.[3] Similarly, the ECtHR has frequently used this Article in the context of other environmental claims. By repeatedly using Article 8 ECHR to adjudicate both housing and environmental issues, it seems to increasingly interpret the right to a home as including the right to a clean environment if the lack thereof affects the applicant's standard of living. *Solyanik v. Russia* reflects the ECtHR's continuous commitment to a combined assessment of environmental and housing issues.

5 Conclusion

The judgment was given against the background of Russia's leaving the Council of Europe in March this year. According to the Resolution adopted by the ECtHR on the consequences of this decision, this means that Russia will only be bound by the ECHR until September 2022, and the ECtHR will not have jurisdiction over any claims after this point.[4]

3 N. Prilutskaya, 'Fadeyeva v. Russia: A Year and a Half after the ECtHR Judgment', European Human Rights Advocacy Centre (EHRAC) Bulletin, No. 7, 2000, pp. 14-15.

4 A. Buyse, 'ECHR Continues to Apply for Russia until 16 September 2022', ECHR Blog, 23 March 2022, https://www.echrblog.com/2022/03/echr-continues-to-apply-for-russia.html (last accessed 4 August 2023).

Available but Inaccessible: Where the Generic Property Right Meets Special Needs

Kati Vainionpää

1 Introduction

Housing rights play a fundamental role in society by ensuring people have access to, for example, shelter and electricity. They also encompass a social aspect by allowing people to participate in their community. While strict standards have been set to determine the minimum requirements of housing adequacy, the most vulnerable groups are often left outside the scope of protection.

Persons with disabilities form one of these groups, as sometimes laws are not enough to ensure inclusiveness. This problem is often rooted in a lack of assessment of each individual situation, leading authorities to disregard special infrastructural requirements for ensuring accessibility. This paper post examines the results and significance of the case of *Guberina v. Croatia* (application no. 23682/13), where the applicant contested discriminatory practices of national authorities in the European Court of Human Rights (hereinafter: the ECtHR).[1]

2 Events that Led to the Landmark Judgement

The case concerned a family of five seeking a tax exemption in order to access housing appropriate for their youngest child. In 2008, the child was diagnosed with multiple physical and mental disabilities. The apartment building where the family was residing at that point in time had no elevator, meaning that the child was limited in his ability to leave the apartment, particularly as he grew older. The father of the family, the applicant, sought a tax exemption from the Croatian authorities, relying on domestic tax law, which aimed to help people buy a flat or house to meet their housing needs, provided they did not already have another flat or housing. In this case, the applicant argued that he should be eligible for this exemption as his flat did not meet his family's housing needs.

1 ECtHR 22 March 2016, no. 23682/13 (Guberina v. Croatia).

The new home would accommodate the needs of his son and family, despite being slightly more expensive. The domestic courts denied his tax exemption request, asserting that all basic requirements were met in the family's previous flat. Domestic law was applied in a strict manner, and the Croatian authorities said the flat had sufficient space for five residents and completely disregarded other relevant facilities.

Before the ECtHR, the applicant relied on Article 1 of Protocol No. 1 to the European Convention on Human Rights (ECHR), providing protection of property, in conjunction with Article 14 ECHR, prohibiting discrimination on any ground such as sex, race, colour, language, religion, and political or other opinion. The applicant claimed that his family's situation placed them in a disadvantaged position compared to others; thus, he should be eligible for the tax exemption.

3 Significant Characterisation of Disability

Under Article 34 ECHR, the ECtHR may hear applications from any person claiming that a contracting party of the ECHR violated their human rights. However, in this case, the applicant was bringing this application on behalf of his son. The ECtHR made a noteworthy comment in relation to the applicant's right to take this legal action. It concluded that although the applicant was not himself affected by the limitations of the first flat, he was the principal caretaker and therefore had a direct connection to his son.[2] The ECtHR acknowledged the fact that disability affects not just the person with a disability but their entire family or whoever predominantly carries such responsibilities.

When determining whether the applicant's rights under Article 14 ECHR had been infringed upon, the ECtHR stated that the Croatian authorities had applied their property legislation in an overly restrictive way and failed to take into account the accessibility of housing for persons with disabilities. The restrictiveness was exaggerated as it failed to consider specific factors, like the child's limited mobility.[3] Despite Croatia having ratified many international and European legal instruments, which protect the rights of people with disabilities, such as the UN Convention on the Rights of Persons with Disabilities and the EU Charter of Fundamental Rights, the domestic authorities did not take into account these obligations.[4] The ECtHR moreover noted that differential treatment is sometimes required to meet the needs of vulnerable groups so that they get

2 ECtHR 22 March 2016, Guberina v. Croatia, pp. 77-79.
3 Ibid., p. 86.
4 Ibid., p. 92.

as close as possible to practising their rights at the same level as other, non-vulnerable groups.

Discrimination can be both direct, meaning it is clearly readable from the letter of the law, and indirect, where the law is applied in the same way to everyone but leaves opportunities for discriminatory practices. This means that a measure can be discriminatory even when it is not directly aimed at the particular group that suffers the discriminatory effect of the measure. This notion is important for the purposes of expanding the scope of protection in case of *de facto* discrimination, which can be harder to detect, such as in the *Guberina*-case. In this case, it was not the letter of the law but rather the restrictive practices and lack of appropriate exceptions that led to unequal outcomes.

By imposing the same tax exemption conditions on all applicants, Croatian legislation discriminated against persons with disabilities by leaving them in a comparably more disadvantaged position. In the end, the ECtHR had to determine whether the housing conditions were considered 'adequate' for the family in question. Even though the applicant and his family were subjected to the same rules as other Croatians, their needs required domestic authorities to apply differential treatment to secure their right to be equal members of society.[5] Emphasis was put on accessibility and that, in some cases, the standard requirements for adequate housing are not enough in cases concerning people with a disability. In the case of *Guberina*, an elevator was considered a required facility needed to protect the right to accessible housing for a person in a wheelchair. As this special requirement was ignored, the ECtHR found an interference with Article 1 of Protocol No. 1 to the ECHR in conjunction with Article 14 ECHR.[6]

4 The Case That Changed the Concept of Discrimination

The ECtHR noted that accessibility could look different depending on the needs of individual persons. The right to housing must give equality of opportunity to all citizens regardless of their health, age, gender, race, or other such characteristics. The judgement in *Guberina v. Croatia* ensures that other laws, such as the Croatian property legislation in question, must be interpreted in conjunction with disability rights. Before this decision, disability rights had been considered a separate branch of law, and the links between discrimination in housing had not been clearly established. In order to equally protect the housing rights of all persons, different legal rules must work together and have the

5 Ibid., p. 83.
6 Ibid., pp. 98-99.

ability to be stretched to allow all people to participate in their community. This is a fundamental right, and there are no justifications for limiting it – not even when national laws contradict international standards.

The prohibition of discrimination connects to other human rights and can only be accepted when there is a clear justification. Although a person may be advantaged in one way, it does not reduce the disadvantage brought by some other factor. This is why the applicant's financial situation was irrelevant to the ECtHR. On top of the fact that the government did not use it as a justification to deny the original tax exemption request, the nature of the prohibition of discrimination for which the wealth status cannot compensate played a part. The right to equal treatment, in this case, aimed to protect and equalise the position of a disabled person and his caretakers. Disabilities are not dependent on the wealth of the persons concerned, and the experienced disadvantages should be compensated by some support that puts disabled people on the same line as their peers.

5 Conclusion: Impact of the Case

Guberina v. Croatia is essential in recognising the importance of tailored treatment. It is an important reminder that equality does not mean putting everyone in the same circumstances but rather acknowledging the differences in individual needs. The ECtHR clearly demonstrated that disabilities impact the entire support network of the person with a disability rather than just the person directly concerned. By including accessibility as a criterion for adequate housing, this case emphasised the importance of participation in society and how living conditions can have a significant effect on the ability to do so. It sets a standard for EU Member States to interpret their laws in a way that allows for exceptions when their citizen is in an unfavourable position.

Part III
Exit Rights

Introduction to Exit Rights

Michelle Bruijn

This section of the book focuses on exit rights. Echoing the introduction of this book, exit rights refer to the aspects of the right to housing of individuals facing the necessity of leaving their homes, whether voluntary or involuntary. The papers in this section focus on the latter scenario, known as eviction.

The international right to housing is essential to protect people against homelessness and eviction.[1] For instance, it requires state parties to explore alternative solutions prior to carrying out evictions and to offer alternative accommodation to vulnerable people, such as children, elderly, refugees, and minority groups.[2] These exit rights find expression in decisions from international courts and committees, such as the Committee of Economic, Social and Cultural Rights, the Committee on the Rights of the Child, and the European Court of Human Rights. The papers in this section shed light on the level of protection offered by these human rights bodies and reveal how this protection varies in each country, with some jurisdictions offering significantly more protection than others.

National courts play an important role in safeguarding the right to housing, as they often need to decide whether an eviction is just or unjust. Legal research shows that courts struggle with this task, particularly in cases in which a tenant faces eviction from privately rented housing.[3] In such instances, human rights come into play within the legal relationship between two private entities – often a landlord and a tenant. Human rights function horizontally in such cases, creating a scenario where conflicting fundamental rights, such as a landlord's right to property and a tenant's right to housing, necessitate judicial balancing. Conversely, when a public authority initiates the eviction, human rights operate vertically. Here, the judge must evaluate the potential infringement on the right to housing by the state actor. The authors of this

1 C.U. Schmid (Ed.), Tenancy law and housing policy in Europe: towards regulatory equilibrium, Cheltenham, Edward Elgar, 2018.

2 P. Kenna, 'Introduction', in P. Kenna, S. Nasarre-Aznar, P. Sparkes & C.U. Schmid (Eds.), Loss of home and evictions across Europe, Cheltenham, Edward Elgar, 2018, p. 26; C.U. Schmid (Ed.), 2018; J. Hohmann, 'The right to housing', in M. Moos (Ed.), A Research Agenda on Housing, Cheltenham, Edward Elgar, 2019, pp. 15-30.

3 See M. Vols et al., 'Common trends in eviction research: a systematic literature review', in M. Vols & C.U. Schmid (Eds), Houses, Homes and the Law, The Hague, Eleven Publishing, 2019, pp. 1-88; M. Vols & E.D. Kusumawati, 'The International Right to Housing, Evictions and the Obligation to Provide Alternative Accommodation', AsiaPacific Journal on Human Rights and the Law, Vol. 21, No. 2, 2020, pp. 237-269.

section delve into both manifestations of eviction: landlord-tenant law evictions and those initiated by a public authority. As such, the authors of this section contribute to the interpretation and application of exit rights by addressing the relationship between the right to housing and the right to property in landlord-tenant law cases, as well as the relationships between the individual and the state.

A pivotal consideration in the majority of eviction cases revolves around determining the proportionality of the eviction.[4] While defining proportionality may resist a one-size-fits-all interpretation, the papers in this part of the book significantly advance the understanding of the proportionality principle. Topics explored include the impact of eviction on children, the eviction of travellers, issues of segregation and poverty, eviction moratoria during the 2008 financial crisis, illegal housing constructions, evictions related to mega sports events (e.g., Olympic Games), and instances where national policies may be deemed excessively protective of tenancy rights, potentially disproportionately affecting the property rights of landlords. Collectively, these papers underscore the need for housing solutions that are not only legally sound but also characterised by equity.

In summary, the contributions in this section illuminate the nuanced interpretation and application of exit rights, offering insights into the multifaceted dimensions of eviction. These findings provide valuable materials for further refining the conceptual framework of exit rights within the broader discourse on housing rights.

---

4 P. Kenna, S. Nasarre-Aznar, P. Sparkes & C.U. Schmid (Eds.), Loss of home and evictions across Europe, Cheltenham, Edward Elgar, 2018; C.U. Schmid (Ed.), 2018; J. Hohmann, 2019, pp. 15-30; L.M. Bruijn, M. Vols & J.G. Brouwer, 'Home closure as a weapon in the Dutch war on drugs: Does judicial review function as a safety net?', International Journal of Drug Policy, Vol. 51, 2018, pp. 137-147; M. Vols, 'European law and private evictions: property, proportionality and vulnerable people', European Review of Private Law, Vol. 27, No. 4, 2019, pp. 719-752.

To Be Evicted or Not to Be Evicted: Analysing the Effects of the Administrative Decision to Expel Dozens of Residents

Andrei-Fabian Balan

1 Introduction

Discrimination against minority groups such as LGBTQ+, racial and religious groups has been a systematic issue since ancient times. While tremendous progress has been made in protecting these disadvantaged groups, discrimination remains a serious problem. One inarguable example is represented by the situation of the Roma people in Europe.[1] The Roma face discrimination on a widespread scale across Europe and, as a result, most of them live below the poverty level.[2] In addition, research has shown that the Roma are deprived of educational opportunities that other Europeans possess and that Roma children are likely to drop out because of racism in schools. Only one out of four Roma finish school, causing only 20% of Roma adults to be able to read and write.[3] To this day, many Roma are still facing discrimination when looking for a job, healthcare, housing or when in contact with administrative of governmental bodies.[4] This is also evidenced by the case of the European Court of Human Rights (hereafter: the ECtHR) *Yordanova and others v. Bulgaria*.[5]

1 Council of Europe, 'Roma and Travellers: Antigypsyism/Discrimination', Council of Europe, https://www.coe.int/en/web/roma-and-travellers/antigypsyism-/-discrimination (last accessed 31 July 2023).

2 Council of Europe, 'Extreme Poverty Afflicts Many of the 10-12 Million Roma in Europe', Council of Europe, 17 October 2019, https://www.coe.int/en/web/roma-and-travellers/-/extreme-poverty-afflicts-many-of-the-10-12-million-roma-in-europe (last accessed 31 July 2023).

3 Y. Mills, 'Roma People: 10 Ways Europe's Biggest Minority Faces Discrimination', Reuters, 8 April 2019, https://www.reuters.com/article/us-global-roma-rights-idUSKCN1RK01Y (last accessed 31 July 2023).

4 D. Simpson, 'The Roma: A Thousand Years of Discrimination Continues in Europe, Advocates Say', CNN, 25 October 2013, https://edition.cnn.com/2013/10/21/world/europe/roma-discrimination/index.html (last accessed 31 July 2013).

5 ECtHR 24 April 2012, no. 25446/06 (Yordanova and others v. Bulgaria).

2 The Events Leading up to *Yordanova and others v. Bulgaria*

The case *Yordanova and others v. Bulgaria* concerns twenty-three Bulgarian nationals of Roma ethnicity living on the outskirts of Sofia, the capital city of Bulgaria. The group of Roma affected in this case arrived and settled there from the 1960s and 1970s, along with recent arrivals in the 1990s. They manually built the homes in which they lived. These buildings lacked authorisation from the government and did not meet the basic safety requirements. Nevertheless, the government never sought to vacate the area or look for solutions regarding the situation, such as providing adequate housing or discussing conditions under which the Roma would have been allowed to remain on the land.

The land on which the Roma people settled was state-owned by the Sofia municipality. It was later sold to a private investor, and the 180 Roma were subsequently told by the mayor that they had to vacate the area within seven days as their homes would be demolished to clear the site for the new proprietor. The applicants did not comply with this order, which led to multiple attempts to remove the Roma. The group of Roma legally challenged their eviction order and asked the Court of First Instance (the Sofia City Court) to stay their removal pending the legal proceedings. The Court granted their request: the Roma could not be evicted until all legal disputes were settled.

The Sofia City Court eventually ruled that the eviction order was lawful. This claim was later upheld by the Court of Appeal (the Supreme Administrative Court of Bulgaria). The Court deemed the order lawful because the applicants had not shown a valid legal ground for occupying the land. The burden of proof rested on the applicants to seek notarial deeds or to bring civil proceedings to establish the rights to occupy the land.

The group of Roma decided to lodge an appeal with the ECtHR, alleging that their eviction would amount to inhuman and degrading treatment and would violate their right to respect for their homes (Art. 3 and Art. 8 of the European Convention on Human Rights, hereafter: the ECHR). Under pressure from members of the European Parliament, the district mayor had postponed the eviction pending the decision from the ECtHR.

3 ECtHR: Forced Evictions of Roma Community Violate Right to Housing

In their appeal, the applicants stated that the houses in which they lived and where they were registered remained their homes even though they built them unlawfully. Furthermore, the applicants claimed that the government's justification for the eviction order is based on private complaints by non-Roma citizens. According to the applicants, these complaints include terms that clearly show racial prejudice; the private complaints are based on the racial opposition between non-Roma residents and the applicants, seeking the 'return of the Roma to their native places'. The applicants also argued that the government selectively demolished illegal constructions in Bulgaria based on racial profiling. Lastly, the applicants considered that the houses they built constituted their 'possessions' in the sense of Article 1 of Protocol Number 1 of the ECHR.[6]

The government of Bulgaria primarily based its arguments on the fact that the applicants unlawfully occupy state-owned property. As such, the applicants could not claim ownership, as they built makeshift houses that violated construction rules. The government also argued that the buildings pose a sanitary risk, do not meet fire safety requirements, and could collapse. In addition, the government presented the argument that the Roma intentionally stirred tensions and provoked reactions from other ethnic groups to gain popularity and privileged treatment, arguing that they were attempting to incite ethnic hatred.

Firstly, the ECtHR had to examine whether enforcing the removal order would constitute an interference of the applicants' rights within the meaning of Article 8(2) ECHR. The ECtHR stated that the makeshift houses the applicants lived in are indisputably their homes regardless of the lawfulness of settling on that land. Therefore, it logically follows that the enforcement of the removal order would constitute an interference of the applicants' rights.

Afterwards, the ECtHR determined whether the measure pursued a legitimate aim. According to the ECtHR, it is undeniable that seeking to regain possession of unlawfully occupied land is legitimate. Furthermore, the government's argument was strengthened by the lack of sewage and sanitary facilities along with the risk of some of the applicants' homes collapsing.

Lastly, the ECtHR observed whether an interference would be considered necessary in a democratic society. It asserted that an interference would be regarded as such if it answered a pressing social need and if it is was proportionate to the aim pursued. The ECtHR declared that the loss of one's home constitutes "the most extreme form of interference" with a person's right to respect for one's home.[7] Thus, the ECtHR expressed that the State's interest in reclaiming its property should come second to the applicants' right.

---

6 ECtHR 24 April 2012, Yordanova and others v. Bulgaria, p. 91.

7 ECtHR 24 April 2012, no. 25446/06 (Yordanova and others v. Bulgaria), p. 117.

The ECtHR considered that, since the residents have been inhabiting the area for a considerable amount of time, they have developed a connection with the community and have become intertwined with the locals. According to the ECtHR, the principle of proportionality requires that such situations should be treated entirely different from routine cases of removal of an individual from unlawfully occupied property. It further observes that the government failed to look at alternative methods to deal with risks stemming from the lack of basic sanitary and safety requirements in the applicants' houses.

The ECtHR acknowledged that the Bulgarian government adopted a ten-year national programme on housing and the situation of the Roma people to ascertain the prevalent issues faced by the Roma and make improvements. Yet, this and other studies or programmes led to no significant results or measures on the issue of housing for racial minorities. Moreover, the administrative authorities had failed to consider the risk of the applicant's becoming homeless if evicted. The ECtHR found it also problematic that the authorities failed to guarantee shelter for the applicants in case of eviction. Article 8 of the ECHR does not include an obligation to provide housing to applicants, but an obligation to secure shelter to particularly vulnerable individuals may flow from this provision. The government should have taken the underprivileged position of the applicants as a weighty factor in the decision to issue an eviction order. The ECtHR ruled that the forceful eviction of the residents would entail a violation of the right to private life under Article 8 of the ECHR (if the eviction order is being enforced), as the legislation did not require the authorities to examine the proportionality of the eviction and decision-making procedure did "not offer safeguards against disproportionate interference".[8]

4 Conclusion

The case *Yordanova and others v. Bulgaria* has become a landmark case. It shows that adequate housing and social security undoubtedly constitute essential human rights which are intrinsically linked to Article 8 of the ECHR. As such, the ECtHR stresses in its judgement that governments should prioritise providing their citizens with adequate housing instead of focusing on their own interests. The significance of this particular case is accentuated in light of the increasing need for affordable housing in Europe as the real estate market becomes progressively more volatile.

8 Ibid., p. 144.

Although the ECtHR's ruling on this matter was beneficial to the Roma that were threatened with eviction, the circumstances concerning the Roma in Europe remain surprisingly unchanged, as many initiatives that have been commenced at a national level proved to be inefficient.[9] Examples of such attempts can be found in Romania, where Roma are assured to enter university free of tuition and without having to sit any other entrance exams that are generally required of other Romanians.[10] However, this attempt has been notoriously riddled with corruption, since there have been many non-Roma Romanians who have taken advantage of the special places allotted to the Roma through the use of bribery, emphasising the widespread corruption and general lack of care towards the plight of the Roma.[11] Nevertheless, the *Yordanova* case highlights the pressing need for a concerted, definitive effort to ensure housing for all citizens, regardless of their ethnicity, religion, or sexual orientation. It underscores the urgency for a large-scale initiative to improve the housing situation in Europe.

9 National Democratic Institute, 'Regional Roma Initiative', NDI, https://www.ndi.org/regional-roma-initiative (last accessed 31 July 2023).

10 A.A. Shvey, M.S. Flaherty & T.E. Higgins, 'Children Left behind: Roma Access to Education in Contemporary Romania', Crowley Mission Reports, Book 3, 2005, http://ir.lawnet.fordham.edu/crowley_reports/3 (last accessed 31 July 2023).

11 Tolo, 'Secureanu Şi-A Pus Fata Pe Listele Romilor Pentru Că-Şi Dorea Să Intre La Un Liceu De Top Din Bucureşti! "A Aranjat Cu Fiul Mamei Omida!"', Tolo.ro, 8 December 2016, https://www.tolo.ro/2016/12/08/secureanu-si-a-pus-fata-pe-listele-rromilor-pentru-ca-si-dorea-sa-intre-la-un-liceu-de-top-din-bucuresti-a-aranjat-cu-fiul-mamei-omida/comment-page-2/ (last accessed 31 July 2023).

Walking a Tightrope: Balancing the Right to Property with the Right to Housing in the European Court of Human Rights

Emma Bowar

1 Introduction

Over the past several decades, the European Court of Human Rights (hereafter: the ECtHR) has developed a substantial and significant jurisprudence addressing the human rights issues incumbent on the relationship between landlords and tenants. Said relationship has been addressed under both Article 8 of the European Convention on Human Rights (hereafter: the ECHR), which provides for the right to private life and home, as well as Article 1(1) of the ECHR, which contains an explicit right to property, providing for the peaceful enjoyment of one's possessions. Within the ambit of Article 1(1), the landlord-tenant relationship is frequently evaluated as an individual interest (of the landlord) versus a national policy which seeks to promote housing or tenants' rights.[1] This balancing act is illustrated particularly well in the case of *Kasmi v. Albania*, where the ECtHR had to balance the applicants right to property with the public interest of protecting the housing rights of vulnerable tenants.[2]

2 The Events Leading up to *Kasmi v. Albania*

In *Kasmi v. Albania*, the applicant claimed that there had been a violation of his right to property as he believed that he had been denied proper restoration of his property rights following the end of the communist regime in Albania in 1992 and the subsequent privatisation of the housing market. The applicant had inherited the property rights to two buildings from his father, whose property rights were recognised by the Tirana Commission on Property Restitution and Compensation prior to his death. To take

1 European Court of Human Rights, 'Guide on Article 1 of Protocol No. 1 to the European Convention on Human Rights', Council of Europe, 2022, https://www.echr.coe.int/documents/d/echr/Guide_Art_1_Protocol_1_ENG (last accessed 31 July 2023).

2 ECtHR 23 June 2020, no. 1175/06 (Kasmi v. Albania).

possession of his property, the applicant sought the eviction of the tenants. Although the District Court of Tirana initially granted his request in May 2003, the decision was overturned by the Court of Appeal in April 2004. The Court of Appeal held that three of the four tenants were lawfully occupying the flat on the grounds of being legally homeless and therefore entitled to maintain their tenancy. The Supreme Court of Albania upheld the decision of the Court of Appeal in July 2005. In December 2005, the applicant filed a complaint before the ECtHR, alleging a violation under Article 1(1) of the ECHR. In 2010 the tenants died, and the applicant could take possession of his property. Yet, the death of the tenants did not halt the application against the Republic of Albania lodged with the ECtHR.

The State of Albania passed several pieces of legislation after 1992 to facilitate the transition from state-controlled housing to a free market system. These include the Privatisation of State-Owned Dwellings Act (which set out a basic plan of action for handling properties which had no former owner), the State Contribution to Homeless Households Act (which regulated loans and rental allowances paid by the State to homeless households), and the Property Acts of 1993, 2004, and 2006 (which attempted to regulate the relationship between tenants and their new landlords, i.e. the former owners who had regained their property). In 2004 and 2007, the State Contribution to Homeless Households Act and the Privatisation of State-Owned Dwellings Act were consolidated into the Social Programmes for the Housing of Inhabitants of Urban Areas Act. In sum, the State of Albania was working to return nationalised property to its former owners, to assist tenants of the nationalised property over which there were no legitimate claims in becoming property owners themselves, and to transition the remaining tenants to new forms of social housing. It is in this context that the applicant claimed restitution of his property, but as was detailed above, such restitution did not come to fruition until the tenants had passed. Furthermore, due to the Constitutional Court's ruling on the State Contribution to Homeless Households Act, the applicant was unable to raise rent above the rates set in 1993.

3 The ECtHR Rules in Favour of Property Owner

The applicant argued before the ECtHR that his rights under Article 1(1) of the ECHR had been violated, as the interference with his property rights had not been in the public interest and had been disproportionate. In short, he held that there had been no public interest in allowing the tenants to remain in possession of the dwelling, as only one of the legally homeless tenants had continued to reside at the property (the other two were living abroad). Furthermore, he held that the government's general policy allowing tenants to continue living in buildings which former owners had reclaimed was not necessitated by public interest. There were only a few properties in Tirana where this was the situation and, as such, they contributed little to the governments overall housing scheme. Additionally, the applicant argued that the state had failed to prioritise the relocation of these tenants as they were obliged to do under domestic legislation. Even if the ECtHR found that there was a legitimate public interest in the matter, the applicant held that the state had failed to proportionally balance his interest as a property owner against the interest of the tenants, as he had possessed no mechanism to seek the end of the tenancy agreement (following the rejected eviction proceedings) or an increase in the rent to the market value.

The government countered by arguing that the interference in the applicant's property rights had been in pursuit of a legitimate aim, namely the provision of housing to the tenants, many of whom were retirees or low-income, and as such, considered by the State to be particularly vulnerable. Furthermore, in the view of the government, the interference was proportionate, taking into account the complexity of the situation and the temporary nature of the interference, as it awaited the State's action to offer alternative housing to the tenants. This action would have restored the applicant's property rights.

The ECtHR, firstly, sought to clarify which period fell specifically within their purview to review. They considered that only the years between 1996 (when the ECHR entered into force in Albania) and 2010 (when the applicant had regained possession of his property) were relevant for examination. Secondly, the ECtHR affirmed the undisputed points of the case, specifically that there had been an interference with the applicant's right to property, and that that interference had been provided for by domestic legislation.

Thirdly, the ECtHR examined whether or not the interference was in pursuit of a legitimate aim, which the applicant contested. The ECtHR considered that it must give due deference to national authorities on their particular society's needs, and thereby significant leeway on the State's implementation and pursuance of economic and social policy. Furthermore, the ECtHR upheld the interpretation provided by the Constitutional Court of Albania, which stated that the national housing policy aimed to address the housing needs of vulnerable communities in a depleted housing market. As such, the ECtHR determined that the interference with the applicant's rights under Article 1(1) of the ECHR had been in pursuit of a legitimate aim and was in the public interest.

Fourthly, the ECtHR considered whether Albania had adequately balanced the public interest against the applicant's right to property. In this respect, it dedicated itself to whether the interference had forced the applicant to bear an excessive burden of a societal problem disproportionate to his position as an individual. The ECtHR considered that two of the three legally homeless applicants had been living abroad for several years when the applicant had regained his property rights. Thus, their interest as tenants should not be measured. Additionally, the ECtHR gave weight to the fact that the applicant was unable to obtain reasonable rent from the tenants and that, although the government purported the situation was temporary, the tenancy agreement had no time limit. These facts together meant that, once the eviction proceedings were rejected, the applicant had no means to regain possession of his property fully, and thus was left in a state of 'perpetual uncertainty' for a significant period of time.[3]

For these reasons, the ECtHR found that the applicant had been made to bear too excessive a burden of the public housing issue. Accordingly, the ECtHR determined that the interference with the applicant's right to property had not been a proportionate measure as regards the aim being pursued, and as such, there had been a violation of Article 1(1) of the ECHR. Having determined that there had been a violation, the ECtHR awarded the applicant 30,000 euros in accordance with Article 41 of the Convention. Given that the judgment was finalised in 2020 and the tenants had passed away in 2010 (allowing the applicant to regain possession of his property) the decision had little impact on the domestic situation.

4 CONCLUSION

In *Kasmi v. Albania*, the ECtHR ruled in favour of the landlord, predominantly because it considered the measures taken by Albania to be disproportionate to their stated aims. This decision reflects the pattern evident in the ECtHR's jurisprudence on Article 1(1) of the ECHR and national housing measures: many of them are decided based on proportionality.[4] For example, in the cases *Hutten-Czapska v. Poland*,[5] *Bittó and others v. Slovakia*,[6] and *Statileo v. Croatia*,[7] which relate to rent control schemes imposed by the state after the fall of a communist regime, the ECtHR ruled that such measures disproportionately impacted the landlords, and as such, violated their property rights. The ECtHR came to a similar conclusion under very different socioeconomic circumstances in *Lindheim and others v. Norway*.[8] In this case, the ECtHR ruled that

3 ECtHR 23 June 2020, Kasmi v. Albania, at 83.
4 European Court of Human Rights, 2022, https://www.echr.coe.int/documents/d/echr/Guide_Art_1_Protocol_1_ENG (last accessed 31 July 2023).
5 ECtHR 19 June 2006, no. 35014/97 (Hutten-Czapska v. Poland).
6 ECtHR 28 January 2014, no. 30255/09 (Bittó and others v. Slovakia).
7 ECtHR 10 July 2014, no. 12027/10 (Statileo v. Croatia).
8 ECtHR 12 June 2012, nos. 13221/08 and 2139/10 (Lindheim and others v. Norway).

the legislation which permitted tenants to renew their lease on their holiday homes indefinitely resulted in a disproportionate disadvantage to the landlords' position.

However, the test of proportionality not only protects landlords but also serves to protect the rights of tenants within the scope of Article 8 of the ECHR. The ECtHR has ruled that under Article 8, domestic authorities are required to ensure that any eviction constitutes a proportionate measure. Failure to uphold this proportionality requirement leads to a violation of the tenant's rights under Article 8 of the Convention.[9]

This dual function of proportionality (i.e. to protect both landlords' property rights and tenant's housing rights) reflects the overarching approach of the ECtHR: it has a firm belief that the ECHR offers tangible rights to individuals, and it is the ECtHR's responsibility to effectively protect these rights.[10] Balancing landlords' rights with tenants' rights within the scope of the ECHR has proven to be a delicate task. Some scholars have been critical of the seemingly inconsistent way in which the ECtHR has applied Article 1(1) of the ECHR.[11] Be that as it may, the ECtHR has been challenged with finding solutions amidst complex societal dramas and complicated fact patterns.[12]

9 See, e.g., ECtHR 21 September 2010, no. 37341/06 (Kay and others v. the United Kingdom); ECtHR 9 October 2003, nos. 39665/98 and 40086/98 (Ezeh and Connors v. the United Kingdom).

10 See also K. Trykhlib, 'The Principle of Proportionality in the Jurisprudence of the European Court of Human Rights', EU and Comparative Law Issues and Challenges Series (ECLIC), Vol. 4, 2020, pp. 128-154.

11 See, e.g., R. Lang, 'Unlocking the First Protocol: Protection of Property and the European Court of Human Rights', Human Rights Law Journal, Vol. 29, No. 6-9, 2008, pp. 205-215.

12 A. Grgić et al., The Right to Property under the European Convention on Human Rights (Human Rights Handbook No. 10), Strasbourg, Council of Europe, 2007.

Ben Djazia's Children before the Committee on the Rights of the Child

Phoebe Muir, Sarah Manohar and Roos Wind

1 Introduction

When parents are being evicted, minor children have no choice but to leave with them. The case of *Ben Djazia et al. v. Spain*, before the Committee of Economic, Social and Cultural Rights (hereafter: ESCR committee), exemplifies this.[1] It concerns the eviction of a married couple and their two young children. During the committee's assessment of whether Spain failed its positive obligation to ensure the right to adequate housing, laid down in Article 11, para. 1 CESCR, the role of the minors serves as an exacerbating factor against the State. However, whilst the children's involvement is seen as an important element of the case, it does not show them to be (socioeconomic) rights holders independently of the family unit.

Yet, the Convention on the Rights of the Child makes it clear that children are independent bearers of rights. In General Comment No. 21, the Committee on the Rights of the Child (CRC committee) even highlights that children in street situations are right holders.[2] Therefore, the question arises if the case would lead to a different outcome if Ben Djazia went to the CRC committee, instead of the ESCR committee. A starting point to answer this is identifying whether the CRC provides a legal basis for a complaint procedure regarding an eviction and if so, how the committee would approach this.

2 Legal Ground for the Eviction Procedure

The CRC committee states in General Comment No. 21 that: 'the right to housing is an important component' of Article 27 CRC. This provision is the only one in the

1 UN Committee on Economic, Social and Cultural Rights (CESCR) 20 June 2017, Communication no. 005/2015 (Ben Djazia et al. v. Spain).

2 UN Committee on the Rights of the Child (CRC), 'General Comment No. 21 (2017) on children in street situations', 21 June 2017, CRC/C/GC/21.

Convention that mentions the word housing. It could likely serve as the legal ground to start a complaint procedure. After all, although research literature on children's rights does not (often) speak of a right to housing within Article 27 CRC, the committee clearly does. According to them, it imposes an obligation upon States to 'take appropriate measures to assist parents and others responsible' for children in realising their right to an adequate standard of living, 'particularly with regard to … housing'. The committee says that this assistance must also be given directly to children. To explain what 'the right to housing' contains, they refer to the ESCR committee. In fact, they even have an eye for the case law of the committee regarding this topic.

3 Ben Djazia Would Be Inadmissible before the CRC Committee

Interestingly, the CRC committee mentions the case of Ben Djazia et al. in the concluding observations for the combined fifth and sixth periodic reports of Spain 2018 when addressing the 'standard of living', reflected in Article 27 CRC.[3] Apart from the fact that this indicates that the committee has attention for the case, it also supports the idea that Ben Djazia could invoke Article 27 CRC as a legal basis in a complaint procedure before the CRC committee. Unfortunately, we will never know if Ben Djazia would be successful since the case would be inadmissible. The events happened namely before the Optional Protocol to the Convention on the Rights of the Child on a communications procedure took effect.[4] However, if Mr Djazia were able to complain before the CRC committee on behalf of his children, they would likely reason in line with the views of the ESCR committee as they already – emphatically – do in the periodic report.

4 A Judgement in Line with the ESCR Committee

In the concluding observations – as mentioned earlier – the CRC committee recommends Spain to improve the national social protection systems by urging to strengthen comprehensive policies for children and their families, specifically focusing on those at risk and needing most support. The committee explicitly recommends strengthening support for families that face eviction due to financial difficulties. They recall the views of the ESCR committee in the case Ben Djazia, to ensure that special attention is paid to evictions involving children.

3 UN Committee on the Rights of the Child (CRC), 'Concluding observations Spain', 9 February 2018, CRC/C/ESP/CO/5-6.

4 See UN Committee on Economic, Social and Cultural Rights (CESCR) 25 January 2018, Communication no. 010/2017 (S.C.S. v. France).

Ben Djazia and his family became homeless. Spanish authorities offered shelter, but this would separate the family. The ESCR committee focuses particularly on the specific care children require, as they can be considered one of the more vulnerable groups in society. This weighs heavily, and consequently, the emphasis on the family unit being supported and kept together to avoid adverse effects on the children forms a key part of the reasoning that led to the committee finding there was a failure on Spain's side.

If the case was admissible before the CRC committee, these views likely would be included in the judgment. This time, they required rather than recommended that Spain implement them. Yet, the approach of the CRC and CESCR differ. Therefore, a reference to the ESCR committee seems insufficient. Hence, the question of how the committee would handle the children's right to housing in an eviction case is not yet answered.

5 The CRC Committee's Approach

The CRC committee says that children suffer disproportionately from forced evictions and that security of tenure is essential to prevent children from becoming homeless and exposing them to further violations of their rights. Whilst we already established that the committee would likely reason in line with the ESCR committee, it's unclear how they would interpret Article 27 CRC in an eviction case. There is a lack of information regarding how the committee interprets the right to housing within the CRC, let alone what role it plays in eviction cases. There is a lacuna in case law. Article 27 CRC has been invoked once before, regarding a forced eviction. Still, the complaint was inadmissible.[5] The holistic nature of the Convention – which the committee highlights in General Comment No. 21 – increases the complexity, as other provisions may also play a role within this case. For example, Article 6 CRC: the right to life, survival and development, since Article 27 CRC seems to be linked to development. Given the committee's holistic children's rights approach, it is not inconceivable that they will include other provisions in their reasoning and in their explanation regarding Article 27 CRC.

6 Concluding

Ben Djazia would be inadmissible before the CRC committee. If this was not the case, Article 27 CRC could likely serve as a legal ground to start a complaint procedure before the CRC committee regarding the forced eviction. The committee will reason in line

5 See CESCR 25 January 2018, S.C.S. v. France.

with the ESCR committee, but what the actual outcome would be remains unclear. It requires more research to determine how the CRC committee interprets Article 27 CRC in an eviction case and which other provisions may play a role in the deliberation.

The Right to Property during an Eviction Moratorium: ECtHR's Steady-Handed Approach in *Béla Németh v. Hungary* Shows the Way for Pandemic Case Pile

Maria Niemelä

1 Introduction

In attempts to solve the emerging housing crisis resulting from the COVID-19 pandemic, some countries, like the United States and Spain, have introduced moratoria on evictions. If past housing crises have taught us anything, it is that a moratorium is effective in the protection of the community but is barely a one-size-fits-all approach: a clash between the interests of the owner of an apartment and tenant is inevitable. It is possible that the European Court of Human Rights (hereafter: the ECtHR) took the pandemic into account when it decided on the conflict in *Béla Németh v. Hungary* in December 2020.[1] The case epitomises the stand-off between two human rights – the right to peaceful possession of property and that of home and private life – in the wake of a legislative moratorium on evictions during the foreign currency loan crisis of 2014.

2 The Case *Béla Németh v. Hungary*

Even years later, the ripple effects of the 2008 financial crisis were rattling the governments of Europe. In Hungary, this took the form of defaulted foreign currency loans. By Rabobank's estimate, 1.1 million Hungarians were struggling to manage their foreign loan payments in 2010.[2] Four years later, the Hungarian government decided to prevent the emerging housing crisis by introducing a moratorium on evictions until further notice. The effects of this were felt by the applicant, who had recently purchased

1 ECHR 17 December 2020, No. 73303/14 (Béla Németh v. Hungary).
2 M. Tömöri and I. Süli-Zakar, 'The State of the Hungarian Residential Market in the Time of the Global Economic Crisis', Revue belge de géographie, No. 3-4, 2011, pp. 167-186.

an apartment, whose former owner was indebted with foreign currency loans. As the former owner was still residing in the apartment on the day the moratorium was issued, no eviction proceedings could be taken against him. This resulted in the inability of the applicant to take possession of the property belonging to him.

Even years later, the ripple effects of the 2008 financial crisis were rattling the governments of Europe. Thus, the applicant invoked Article 1 of Protocol No. 1 European Convention on Human Rights (hereafter: the ECHR), by claiming that the government interfered with the peaceful enjoyment of his possession (i.e. the residential property). He claimed the amendment to the law was unlawful, partly due to the uncertainty caused by the moratorium, as the measure was initially introduced with no specific time limit. In doing so, he alleged that given the fact that the financial crisis only affected a portion of the population, it was not enough to trigger public interest. In addition, the applicant questioned the fairness of the conditions of the moratorium. According to the applicant, there was a lack of countermeasures he could have taken while waiting for the eviction proceedings to resume, such as retracting his bid on the property. He particularly scrutinised the condition for being excepted from the measure since such a clause was only available to the State's economic operators. According to the applicant, this amounts to discrimination towards private actors under Article 14 ECHR.

The government contested these arguments. Whereas the financial crisis did not concern all of the Hungarian population, the amount and severity were still significant to trigger public interest. The uncertainty of the moratorium (caused by the unspecified time limit) could be explained by the uncertainty caused by the crisis itself. Additionally, the government presented the ECtHR with the applicant's status regarding the apartment as noted in the land registry; instead of being associated as the owner, his claim to the apartment was documented under 'auction buyer'. With this in mind, the government posited that the aforementioned fact negated legitimate expectations that only an owner could have towards the property.

3 The Court's Decision

The applicant's status of ownership was verified by the ECtHR, who declared that legitimate expectations had been raised due to the rightful belief that proper registration of status would happen following payment. As evident, the inability of the applicant to take action resulted in an interference by the State of his right. The point of contention was thus whether the interference was justified. For this to be the case, the weight of public interest, the domestic law, and the general principles of international law were analysed with special regard to the criteria of pursuing a legitimate aim and striking a fair balance between housing rights and property rights.

In deciding the matter, the ECtHR first noted that the basis for the measure in domestic law was never declared unconstitutional. Therefore, the restriction to the applicant's right was subjected to conditions provided for by law. Secondly, the moratorium pursued a legitimate aim, namely the prevention of a multitude of evictions, as well as the prevention of irreversible harm to consumers resulting from unfair loan terms. Thirdly, the ECtHR ruled that the moratorium was proportionate. Due to the wide margin of appreciation granted to States under Article 1 Protocol No. 1, it is noted in case law that a system that momentarily freezes court proceedings but later on allows the reinstatement of a landlord in his property is not inherently unlawful.[3] Consequently, ownership was merely delayed, not denied, which is permitted under the second paragraph of Article 1: it contains the rule that the State should be able to control the use of property while enforcing laws, which in this case points to the moratorium.

For the reasons discussed above, the effects of the moratorium on the applicant were justified. While it was true that the moratorium had no end-date initially, this was set through subsequent legislation that was passed at most seven months after evictions were frozen. Thus, because the uncertainty did not persist and the interference was limited, no violation was found to the applicant's right to peaceful enjoyment of possessions under Article 1 of Protocol No. 1.

Finally, the applicant resorted to Article 14 of the ECHR (prohibition of discrimination) stating that the moratorium did not apply to State actors. According to the applicant, this was discriminatory, as he could have undertaken similar actions to that of the State, such as offering subsidised housing to workers. The government disagreed, arguing that the functions performed by State entities while representing the public interest could not be achieved on the same scale in the private sector. As State measures can be seen as a reflection of a more general social policy – and in this case, the preservation of rural communities – the government successfully asserted that differential treatment was justified in the light of the wide margin of appreciation afforded to States. For the lack of demonstration on the applicant's part that their situation was comparable to that of the State, the ECtHR dismissed the applicant's claim.

3 See, e.g., ECHR 25 March 1999, No. 31107/96 (Iatridis v. Greece).

4 Conclusion

Sometimes, ensuring the effectiveness and practicality of the human right to housing means that other individual rights are compromised, such as the right to property, as in *Béla Németh v. Hungary*. The ideology behind the right to property may explain its position as a secondary priority: it is argued that the right to property only exists when necessary for subsistence (see American Declaration on the Rights and Duties of Man, Article XXIII). The very same rationale may lie behind the loophole in the current moratorium in force in the United States, where eviction proceedings are possible during such a moratorium if the landlord or their close family move to the property in question.[4] The trend insinuating that property rights should aim to uphold basic subsistence is also present in the ECtHR's case law.[5]

With this in mind, it is surprising that the judgement did not further inspect the economic position of the applicant in determining the magnitude of the individual burden. It is unclear if the applicant wished to move into the property himself during the two years of the moratorium and whether he would have been compensated. This shows some hesitation on the part of the ECtHR to recognise an independent right to subsistence. The lack of analysis on the economic position of the applicant may be explained through the proportionality test – the protection of subsistence through the right to property is not guaranteed but likely to be taken into account in said test.[6] In the case at hand, maintaining the right to a home for as many people as possible outweighed these concerns. Until this day, foreign currency loans remain in Hungarian headlines and have facilitated the effects of the COVID-19 pandemic, leading to another moratorium that has only recently been lifted.[7] By showing the importance and weight of the right to housing during a national emergency, the case *Béla Németh v. Hungary* will undoubtedly be significant case law for the future cases of the pandemic.

4 K. Klein, 'Landlord Wants to Move into Rental Property', StarTribune, 30 April 2021.

5 ECHR 10 February 2015, No. 53080/13 (Béláné Nagy v. Hungary).

6 I. Leijten, 'The Right to Minimum Subsistence and Property Protection under the ECHR: Never the Twain Shall Meet?' European Journal of Social Security, Vol. 21, No. 4, 2019, pp. 307-325.

7 V. Gulyas, 'Hungary Extends Eviction Moratorium for Forex Debtors', The Wall Street Journal, 14 May 2014.

Red Card for Forced Evictions Related to Mega Sports Events

Maria Niemelä

1 Introduction

The home is at the centre of the actualisation of many human rights. In the famous words of Sir Edward Coke, "[e]veryone's house is his safest refuge".[1] Article 17 of the International Covenant on Civil and Political Rights stipulates that "[n]o one shall be subjected to arbitrary or unlawful interference with his privacy, family, home or correspondence", and further that "[e]veryone has the right to the protection of the law against such interference or attacks".

The origins of the right to privacy are said to lie with the right to property, which worked to demarcate the physical boundaries of the developing concept of the personal, private sphere.[2] Lockean philosophy concerning the social contract views one's property as a means for individuals to be free from state interference while still being subjects of the law.[3] State interference is thus allowed to the extent permitted by law, which is drafted by the legislature representing the will of the majority. According to Locke, power must only be used for the public good.[4]

2 The Impact of Sports Events on Housing and Human Rights

Recently, the international community was reminded of the impact mega sports events can have on the private lives of individuals living in the hosting country. Hosting big global events such as the Olympic Games and the FIFA World Cup comes with a need to make space for accommodation and transportation infrastructure, which often comes at the expense of private property and the housing rights of many.[5] Often, the

1 E. Coke, Selected Writings and Speeches (ed. S. Sheppard), Indianapolis, Liberty Fund, 2003.
2 S. DaCosta, 'Privacy-as-Property: A New Fundamental Approach to the Right to Privacy and the Impact This Will Have on the Law and Corporations', Master Thesis, 2021.
3 J. Locke, Second Treatise of Government, 1689, https://web.archive.org/web/20070304114414/http://oregonstate.edu/instruct/phl302/texts/locke/locke2/locke2nd-a.html (last accessed 2 August 2023).
4 Ibid.
5 L. Oleniacz, 'Human Rights Take Spotlight Ahead of World Cup in Qatar', NCSU, 17 November 2022.

criminalisation of homelessness and informal activities, displacement, and the lack of alternative housing takes place in connection to these events.[6] A particularly serious form of interference takes place when a person is forcibly evicted from their home or settlement.

3 Development-based Evictions

The evictions taking place in connection to mega sports events are argued to be development-based evictions,[7] meaning that they are often said to be conducted to serve the interests of the public, and therefore, in accordance with Lockean standards for justified state interference.

What has been said internationally about such evictions is that they must only be undertaken in exceptional circumstances and for the sole purpose of promoting the general welfare.[8] The accruing general welfare must be evident, and the steps taken by States must be consistent with their overall international human rights obligations, or otherwise they will qualify as forced evictions and, thus, gross violations of international human rights law.[9]

4 Forced Evictions?

The prohibition of forced evictions follows from Article 11(1) of the International Covenant on Economic, Social and Cultural Rights, which guarantees the right to adequate housing. They can be defined as

> [t]he permanent or temporary removal against their will of individuals, families and/or communities from the homes and/or land which they occupy, without the provision of, and access to, appropriate forms of legal or other protection.[10]

---

6 UN Human Rights Council (HRC), Report of the Special Rapporteur on Adequate Housing as a Component of the Right to an Adequate Standard of Living, and on the Right to Non-discrimination in this Context, A/HRC/13/20, United Nations, 2009.

7 UN Human Rights Council (HRC), Annex 1 of the Report of the Special Rapporteur on Adequate Housing as a Component of the Right to an Adequate Standard of Living, A/HRC/4/18, United Nations, 2007.

8 HRC, 2007.

9 UN Commission on Human Rights, Prohibition of Forced Evictions Commission on Human Rights, Resolution: 2004/28, United Nations, 2004.

10 UN Committee on Economic, Social and Cultural Rights (CESCR), General Comment No. 7: The Right to Adequate Housing (Art.11.1): Forced Evictions, 20 May 1997, E/1998/22.

The issue with mega sports events is that the provision of legal or other protection against forced eviction may exist in the form of a legal basis as required by Lockean standards for state interference, but the law may not be appropriate by definition of international human rights standards. Contrary to popular belief, forced evictions may still take place even if they happen pursuant to the law. The preparations for mega sports events often involve the promulgation of special laws that grant authorities the power to evict in the public interest. For example, prior to the Sochi Olympics in Russia in 2014, Law 301 acted as the legal basis for clearing the area of over 1,000 homes to create space for sports facilities, resulting in an interference with the private lives of many.[11]

Evictions should only take place when they are unavoidable.[12] Therefore, the access to legal and other protection becomes of great importance in the protection of individual rights.[13] It is essential that when eviction takes place that the evictees receive fair compensation and, more importantly, alternative housing.

5 CONCLUSION

Mega sport events have enormous potential to interfere with (or even violate) the private lives of people and their rights to security of the home. One can wonder if these interferences are always pursuing the public interest and if they promote general welfare. Forced removals especially intersect with the protection of human rights, such as the right to property and the right to housing. States hosting mega sport events should be aware of the thin line between promoting and facilitating the event and violating human rights. Behind all the glamour, global sport events often leave behind a shadow legacy of damage to vulnerable people.

11 L.C. Crout, 'Forced Evictions, Homelessness, and Destruction: Summer "Games"? Olympic Violations of the Right to Adequate Housing in Rio de Janeiro', Notre Dame Journal of International & Comparative Law, Vol. 8, No. 1, 2018, pp. 36-53.

12 UN Habitat & OHCHR, Forced Evictions. Fact Sheet No. 25/Rev. 1, New York, United Nations, 2014.

13 Ibid.

THE RIGHT TO HOUSING VERSUS DEVELOPMENT PROJECTS: THE CASE OF *FAULKNER AND MCDONAGH V. IRELAND*

Emma Sweeney

1 INTRODUCTION

Demovictions and renovictions have been on the rise in recent years. Demovictions refer to evictions that are carried out due to the landowners wish to demolish the property. Renovictions are evictions that are carried out when the landowner wishes to renovate the property. The relationship between evictions and property turnover and redevelopment has emerged as an important dimension in eviction research. Many landowners are evicting Roma and Traveller communities in order to carry out development projects. This leads to the perpetuation and amplification of socioeconomic inequalities in vulnerable communities. These evictions further intensify the discrimination, rejection, social exclusion, and marginalisation they face in all aspects of life, including in housing. This is evidenced in the cases of *Faulkner v. Ireland* and *McDonagh v. Ireland* (App. 30391/18 and 30416/18).

2 DEVELOPMENT PLANS AND THE EVICTION

The applicants, who are sisters and members of the Travelling Community, were illegally occupying a roadside site in Coonagh, Limerick from 2013 to 2017. Limerick City and County Council (the local authority responsible for improving and maintaining regional and local roads) were granted planning permission to build a new ring road around Limerick city to alleviate traffic congestion in the city. The Coonagh site was located in an area where the new road would be located.

In 2017, the Council initiated proceedings to have the applicants and other people living on the site evicted in order to begin the roadwork. The Council engaged a contractor to carry out the roadwork. However, the applicants continued to live on the site. This caused construction delays, during which the building contractors claimed large sums of money from the Council as they had failed to make the location suitable for the development project. The Council obtained orders from the Irish Circuit Court and High Court for the site to be vacated.

During the Circuit Court proceedings, the applicants, who had limited financial means, did not have legal representation. Despite the lack of representation, the Court ordered them to leave the site. Several weeks later, the applicants obtained legal aid, and applied to have the orders suspended to allow sufficient time to find another place to live. The Circuit Court declined this request, only allowing for a few additional days for the applicants to vacate the site. The applicants did not leave the site on the required date. They issued two appeals before the High Court. However, the High Court upheld the original order as it was satisfied that the Circuit Court had dealt with the matter correctly and noted that the applicants had been offered alternative accommodation. However, the judge stated that it was not for him to decide if the applicant had refused the accommodation with good reason or not. Consequently, the High Court did not consider the suitability of the offered alternative accommodation. In carrying out the balancing exercise, the High Court identified the essential interests at play: the applicant's prospects for alternative accommodation, the substantial losses that the local authority would accrue as a result of the delay, and the public interest in the improvement of the local road system.

3 The European Court of Human Rights Decision

Having failed in their appeals in the national courts, the applicants brought their case before the European Court of Human Rights (ECtHR). Due to the similarities in subject matter, the ECtHR decided to examine the applicants jointly. In both cases, the Court was tasked with balancing the applicants' Article 8 rights (the right to respect for private and family life, home and correspondence) with the State's development plans.

The applicants argued that the domestic courts had failed to assess the proportionality test of the eviction orders, which is required under Article 8 (para. 2) of the European Convention on Human Rights (the Convention), and that the domestic court proceedings were conducted with undue haste, without any legal representation at the court hearings.

Ms Faulkner alleged that the State had not offered her suitable alternative accommodation. She claimed that the accommodation that was offered was unsuitable due to the trauma she had suffered due to the deaths of two of her five children, one due to suicide. She wished to raise her remaining children in a safe and rural community. The State asserted that family space on a halting site had been offered to the applicant but that the applicants rejected this.

Ms McDonagh's family had been provided with emergency accommodation in a hotel in July 2017. They lived in the hotel for a period of time, but issues such as the lack of cooking facilities and the long distance between the hotel and the child's school were having an increasingly negative effect on their mental and physical health, particularly that of her husband, who suffered from depression. They eventually returned to living on the site. The State did not argue about the suitability of the accommodation but maintained that the applicant still had access to this emergency accommodation at the time of the domestic legal proceedings and would not be rendered homeless as a result of the eviction.

The ECtHR ruled that the roadside site in Coonagh, where the applicants lived, qualified as home for the purposes of Article 8 of the European Convention and that there had been an interference with these rights. The Court held that this interference was in accordance with law and pursued a legitimate aim as the local authority aimed to improve the economic well-being of the country through the improvement of the road networks and to ensure the personal safety of those onsite at the roadwork.

The key question that remained for the ECtHR was if the interference was 'necessary in a democratic society. When assessing this, the Court investigated if the State's action pursued a pressing social need and if it had been proportionate to the relevant aims. The ECtHR affords the national authorities a 'margin of appreciation' to allow them space in fulfilling their obligations under the Convention. The leniency of this margin varies according to the nature of the right at hand, the importance to the individual, and the nature of the activities restricted. The Court is required to examine if the decision-making process leading to the interference was fair and if it respected the individual's Article 8 rights.

In its decision, the ECtHR noted that the loss of one's home is the most extreme interference with Article 8, and the victim is entitled to have an independent tribunal assess the proportionality of the measure. Where proportionality concerns are raised at domestic judicial proceedings, the Court noted that the domestic court must examine the arguments in detail and provide adequate reasons. In particular, the Court noted that the availability of alternative accommodation should be considered and that the more suitable the alternative accommodation the less serious the interference would be. The ECtHR said as the applicants' status as members of the Travelling Community is a relevant factor in this case and that special consideration must be given to their needs and their different lifestyle.

In coming to its final decision, the ECtHR made three main points:
1. It found that the decisions made by the Circuit Court and the High Court reflected the essential principles of Article 8 of the Convention, particularly in regard to proportionality. The ECtHR reviewed the relevant decisions of the Irish Supreme Court that the Circuit Court and the High Court had cited in the proceedings. Those cases had

all been decided by reference to the Convention principles and referred to relevant case law of the European Court, namely the Chapman decision.

2. The ECtHR found that while the applicants may have been disadvantaged by their lack of legal representation during the Circuit Court proceedings, they were directly heard in the court on that occasion and were able to explain their disadvantaged personal circumstances. The Court highlighted that the issue of legal representation was solved quickly and that the applicants had legal representation at the High Court. Additionally, the High Court had accurately identified and balanced the essential interests at play: the applicant's prospects for alternative accommodation, the substantial losses that the local authority would accrue as a result of the delay, and the public interest in the improvement of the local read system. In addition, the applicant's occupation of the site had been illegal, meaning that their position was regarded as 'less strong' than people living in a legal settlement. The Court decided that in light of the facts of this case and given that the proportionality of the interference was examined judicially, the respondent State had remained within its margin of appreciation.

3. The ECtHR noted that its role is not to sit as an appeals court on the merits of the order but to verify whether domestic authorities remained in their margin of appreciation. The Court held that the State had a wide margin of appreciation as the construction of roads and the availability of suitable alternative accommodation provided by local authorities fall within the sphere of social policy and involve the allocation of public resources, indicating that a broader margin of appreciation should be allowed.

In light of the above three factors, the ECtHR held that the applicant's arguments were inadmissible. The Court found no basis to find that the court orders to vacate the Coonagh site had been disproportionate to the legitimate aim pursued, which was to improve infrastructure and public safety. Hence, the ECtHR ruled that there was no violation.

4 Comment

This case highlights the difficulties the ECtHR faces in carrying out an effective proportionality analysis when an individual's right to housing comes into conflict with States' development plans. In this case, the Court noted that the Irish High Court had carried out a balancing exercise; however, it noted that this was 'not as detailed' as it would have been if the applicants had pursued a different legal argument. Notably, in carrying out the proportionality test, the High Court judge stated that it was not for the court to decide if the applicant had refused the accommodation with good reason or not. However, given the vulnerable position of members of the Travelling Community in Ireland, an assessment of the suitability of the alternative accommodation should have been integral to this balancing exercise. This is made more pertinent considering that the applicants had children in local schools, and the second applicant's husband's mental health challenges. Furthermore, the ECtHR noted that domestic courts should look at the availability of alternative accommodation and that the more suitable the accommodation, the less serious the interference would be. However, this suitability requirement was not thoroughly investigated by the High Court.

5 Conclusion

This case highlights the difficulties facing vulnerable households, particularly including members of the Travelling Community, when landowners decide to carry out demovictions and renovictions. This case suggests that proportionality is difficult to assess in relation to development projects as the rights of individuals are in conflict with possible benefits for the society as a whole. These are difficult interests for the ECtHR to measure and balance. This is particularly true in cases such as Faulkner and McDonagh where the applicants were not living in a legal settlement but where the eviction would have served as a device to amplify social and economic inequalities, particularly due to the lack of suitable and long-term alternative accommodation.

The Individual and State Interest Opposed in Azerbaijan's Illegal Construction Crisis: Proportionality as the Starting Point of Humane Justice

Maria Niemelä

1 Introduction

Ahmadova v. Azerbaijan (App. No. 9437/12) is a property case, decided by the European Court of Human Rights (hereinafter: the ECtHR) on the 18th of November, 2021.[1] The ECtHR was tasked with balancing the applicant's home and family life rights with the State's oil company, Azneft's, industrial interests, and property rights. The applicant's home was built on what was seemingly state-owned land, according to a City Council document dating back to 1962, when Azerbaijan was still a Soviet Republic. The case highlights the decades of uncertainty in the housing sector that followed Azerbaijan's separation from the Soviet Union.

This legal uncertainty caused an illegal construction crisis, which is rooted in the privatisation of property. In its first phase, the State's policy was to freely hand out property and land to people, with no further information on the legal and financial implications of such transfers. The regulatory environment was unclear as Soviet law was still in use. As a result, many took matters into their own hands instead of initiating the lengthy procedure of obtaining a building permit, and many families resorted to illegal constructions.[2]

The most common cases occur either by illegally extending permitted buildings or, like in the applicant's case, squatting on another's land, without the necessary permits. This

1 ECtHR 18 November 2021, No. 9437/12 (Ahmadova v. Azerbaijan).

2 United Nations Economic Commission for Europe, Country Profiles on Housing Sector: Azerbaijan, New York, United Nations, 2010.

case sets an important precedent for domestic courts on how to deal with the extensive illegal construction crisis, while respecting the tenants' human rights.

2 Facts and Domestic Law

The applicant and her daughter resided in an unauthorised construction on state-owned land, assigned for petroleum operations by Azneft. In 2010, Azneft commenced proceedings against the applicant, with the intention of evicting the tenants and demolishing the building concerned. The civil code of Azerbaijan regulates the position of those living in unauthorised properties as follows: pursuant to Section 1, Article 180 (Section 2), the person in charge shall be unable to obtain the title of ownership and rights conferred therefrom. Under Section 4, a court may order for the demolition of the property. The applicant could not claim to have made the purchase in good faith – her ownership had not been appropriately registered and approved by a notary, as required by the constitutive registration system for the transfer of immovables in Azerbaijan. Thus, her occupation of the property was considered squatting on the land, prohibited under Article 111 of the land law. Article 111 authorises the demolition of buildings on squatted land, pursuant to a court order, without compensation. Based on Article 111, in conjunction with the Civil Code, the Sabail District Court issued the order for eviction and the demolition on the grounds that the applicant should have been aware of the illegal nature of the property.

3 The Court

Following fruitless appeals, the applicant submitted the case to the ECtHR for review under Article 1 of Protocol No. 1, peaceful enjoyment of property, in conjunction with Article 8, the right to respect for home and family life, of the European Convention on Human Rights (hereinafter: the Convention). The applicant argued that the demolition of the house, without compensation and at her expense, would amount to a disproportionate interference under Article 1 of Protocol No. 1. The right to peaceful possession of property is not absolute – it can be restricted in cases of public interest, when subject to conditions provided for by law, to be read in light of general principles of law.[3] As a counterargument, the government raised the issue of non-compliance with the requirements for the transfer of immovables. The contract of sale included a section

3 European Court of Human Rights, 'Guide on Article 1 of Protocol No. 1 to the European Convention on Human Rights', Council of Europe, 2022, https://www.echr.coe.int/documents/d/echr/Guide_Art_1_Protocol_1_ENG (last accessed 11 December 2023).

meant for the notary to fill, but it was left blank – a fact pointing to possible awareness concerning the lack of relevant documents. They argued that the land should be vacated, because there should be no residential buildings in an industrial area, as established in a Sabail City Council Decision.

The applicant responded by citing another City Council decision from 2001, which allocated a part of land designated for industrial purposes in 1962 for residential use. The applicant asserted that her house was situated on this plot, among other residential buildings on the land. Her stay in the house and on the land had been acknowledged – which, in turn, had raised reasonable expectations under Article 1 to preserve the status quo. During her stay, there had been no interventions on the part of the authorities. Additionally, the parent company of Azneft, SOCAR, by issuing utility bills to her, had also tolerated her tenancy in the house. Moreover, she argued that evicting her would lead to uncertainty and an interference with the social and family life that she had established in the building.

The ECtHR interprets 'possession' broadly – its definition is not only limited to an existing possession but also covers assets and claims towards which the applicant may have a legitimate or reasonable expectation of obtaining effective enjoyment of a property right.[4] Thus, despite not having the title of ownership under domestic law, the applicant could still enjoy the protection provided by Article 1 of Protocol No. 1, should her expectations fall within the scope of the above-mentioned categories.[5] A legitimate expectation may only be derived from a legal act, meaning it is not applicable to the case. The 'reasonable' criterion requires the circumstances of the case to be considered as a whole, in order to determine whether they conferred a title to a substantive interest on the part of the applicant.

According to the ECtHR, there was no reason for the applicant to believe that the domestic law on the transfer of property would not apply to her. While in the case *Öneryildiz v. Turkey*, which also concerned an eviction on the grounds of an unauthorised construction, the ECtHR took the provision of utility services into account, and in the *Ahmadova* case, the ECtHR did not. There are significant differences between the cases. Firstly, in the present case, the legal status of the house was not still disputed and the applicant had not paid any taxes on the house. Secondly, the demolition order was within a reasonable timeframe and, therefore, was allowed. Finally, the absence of a reaction on the part of the authorities should not have led the applicant to believe that no proceedings could be brought against her. This expectation did not create a

4 European Court of Human Rights, 2022.
5 ECtHR 18 June 2002, No. 48939/99 (Öneryildiz v. Turkey).

substantial and weighty proprietary interest and, thus, failed to amount to a possession within the meaning of Article 1 of Protocol No. 1.

Similarly to the term 'possession', the concept 'home' has an autonomous meaning under Article 8 of the Convention. It is not dependent on the classification established under domestic law and, thus, can entail a wider range of dwellings, whether lawful or not. The determinant factor is the existence of sufficient and continuous links to the building in question. The applicant has established this and, therefore, together with her daughter, she had adequately established that her family life in the house falls within the ambit of Article 8. Despite the fact that the eviction order had not yet been enforced, it remained enforceable, which amounted to an interference of the applicant's rights under Article 8. The Court proceeded to analyse the justifications for the interference.

The above-mentioned articles of the civil code and land law satisfied the ECtHR that the measure was in accordance with the law. Despite the applicant's arguments, the Court held that the interference pursued a legitimate aim, albeit not the economic well-being of the State as argued by the government, but the protection of legitimate interests of Azneft. The interests at stake proceeded to be weighed in the necessity test. The applicant raised the issue of proportionality as the fact her eviction would lead to homelessness was completely ignored by domestic courts. Moreover, SOCAR had neither used the land since 1962 nor was it urgently needed for public use. The Court's case law suggests that mere judicial review is not enough to satisfy due diligence, but rather there should be a real possibility of a case-by-case review.[6] *Yordanova and others v. Bulgaria* listed factors that could be of relevance, including the knowledge of the unlawfulness of the building, the nature and degree of illegality at issue, the interest that is protected by the demolition, and whether there is alternative accommodation available to the persons affected.[7] Overall, the least severe action should be taken, while providing adequate reasons.

In the light of the criteria above, the ECtHR noted that the domestic courts based their judgements solely on the fact that the building was on state-owned land, with no regard to the applicant's personal circumstances; however, the government and Azneft did not argue that the land was urgently needed for industrial operations. Thus, the proceedings at the domestic level failed to give adequate reasons for the proportionality of the measure. No alternative measures were considered; nor was there an opportunity for alternative housing, because the individual did not qualify as a member of a

6 ECtHR 21 April 2016, No. 46577/15 (Ivanova and Cherkezov v. Bulgaria).

7 ECtHR 24 April 2012, No. 25446/06 (Yordanova and others v. Bulgaria). See also the A. Balan, 'To Be Evicted or Not to Be Evicted: Analysing the Effects of the Administrative Decision to Expel Dozens of Residents', in this edited volume.

vulnerable group. However, the ECtHR has previously ruled that the loss of a home is the most serious form of interference, whether the person belongs to a vulnerable group or not.[8] Therefore, the Court held that the eviction and demolition orders were not necessary in a democratic society under Article 8 of the Convention due to the lack of a proportionality review which properly assessed the applicant's personal circumstances.

4 Conclusion

The question whether the house in question was on the plot of former industrial land subsequently allocated to residential purposes was left unresolved. The two pertinent City Council Decisions only raised further questions. Firstly, the 2001 Decision was dismissed by the ECtHR, on the grounds that it was impossible to see whether the house was located on the reallocated plot of land. Secondly, the 1962 Decision to allocate the land for industrial use was approved as late as 2008, a year after the applicant moved in, which may pose a threat to their legal certainty. Moreover, the land allocation system in use when the decision was taken was completely different from the one adopted in the 1990s, and still in use in 2008, both practically and ideologically.[9]

The case is yet another reminder of the importance of a comprehensive proportionality review when it comes to the right to respect for one's home. Personal circumstances weigh heavily in this regard, as a home is of 'central importance' to an individual's physical and moral integrity and a secured place in the community.[10] The State is thought to represent the will of the people, and, in the case of unauthorised constructions, the right to property of others must be protected.

Balancing combating illegal activity and upholding the law with humane justice can be difficult, but the proportionality test provides a way for the ECtHR to come to a fair and reasonable conclusion. For a long time, the State did not establish sanctions for illegal constructions. The consequences can be seen in the architecture of the capital today – approximately 500,000 unauthorised constructions are located in Baku alone.[11] Azerbaijan has recently announced its intention to reform the urban scenery

8 ECtHR 21 April 2016, Ivanova and Cherkezov v. Bulgaria.

9 Asian Development Bank, REG: Mainstreaming Land Acquisition and Resettlement Safeguards in the Central and West Asia Region, 2014, https://www.adb.org/projects/documents/mlars-central-west-asia-azerbaijan-country-assessment-tacr (last accessed 6 March 2024).

10 European Court of Human Rights, Guide on Article 8 of the Convention – Right to Respect for Private and Family Life, Strasbourg, Council of Europe, 2022.

11 United Nations Economic Commission for Europe, 2010.

in the city.[12] One can only wonder what this means to the homes established in times of uncertainty and the physical and moral integrity of the people living there.

12 Trend news agency, 'Illegal Construction Must Be Stopped – President Ilham Aliyev Appeals to Entrepreneurs', Trend News Agency, 3 March 2022, https://en.trend.az/azerbaijan/politics/3563700.html (last accessed 1 December 2023).

Tales from Europe's Largest Garbage Ghetto: Why Ethnic Minorities Are Still Scavenging for Their Right to Adequate Housing

Maria Anghel

1 Introduction

The universal character of human rights, as seen from a morally idealistic point of view, is derived from the equality of men – remnants of this belief transcend the philosophical realm and materialise into legal theory through the prohibition on discrimination inherent in every legal right, thus propelling the idea that the universality of human rights necessarily entails their equal application to all members of society. As such, the right to housing should be construed in such a way that unequivocally precludes bias in its application. And yet, given that the application of law is subject to human error, it is often the case that prejudice alters the effective protection of the right to housing for certain socially disadvantaged communities, such as the Roma community.[1] This paper shall depict the impact of ethnic prejudice on the interpretation of 'adequate housing' by focusing on the human rights crisis in Pata-Rât, Romania. Pata-Rât, the former landfill of Cluj-Napoca, doubles as the largest garbage ghetto in Europe, housing over 1,500 Roma people, many of them having been evicted by the Cluj Municipality from their flats and relocated to the city garbage dump. As such, it provides a poignant image of the dissonance between the legal obligations of Romania regarding the right to housing and its treatment of the Roma minority in connection to this right.

2 The Right to Housing: Rights and Obligations

The right to housing can be understood from two perspectives – not only does it confer upon individuals legal certainty and security against forceful evictions, but it also creates

1 European Union Agency for Fundamental Rights (FRA), 'Housing Conditions of Roma and Travellers in the European Union', FRA, 2009, https://fra.europa.eu/sites/default/files/fra_uploads/703-Roma_Housing_Comparative-final_en.pdf (last accessed 20 November 2023).

a relative standard as to the 'adequacy' of the dwelling. In *Winterstein and others v. France*, the European Court of Human Rights (hereinafter: ECtHR) ruled that eviction measures must pass both a necessity test and a proportionality test in order to sufficiently and effectively protect the rights of the evicted party.[2] Building upon that in *Yordanova and others v. Bulgaria*, the Court contends that the proportionality test creates a positive obligation for the Member States to aid evictees in finding alternative housing – such an obligation is especially paramount in situations concerning vulnerable communities and socially disadvantaged groups.[3] The imminent risk of homelessness for the individual due to the lack of alternative housing has repeatedly been considered a decisive factor in assessing the proportionality of an eviction measure, tipping the scale towards the Court finding a violation of the right to respect for the home (see inter alia *Stankova v. Slovakia*,[4] *Gladysheva v. Russia*[5]).

3 Triggering a Housing Crisis: The Eviction of Seventy-Six Roma Families

On 17 December 2010, the municipal authorities of Cluj-Napoca forcibly evicted seventy-six Roma families from their homes on Coastei Street, by demolishing the blocks of flats in which they resided – the inhabitants were given a one-day notice to vacate the premises, in spite of earlier promises from the municipality that they would not be forced to leave their homes. Moreover, it was contended by the European Roma Rights Centre that the eviction measure lacked legal authorisation.[6] While the official justification for the eviction measure referred to the inhabitants' lack of legal right over the property (as most of the families were residing in the flats on Coastei Street pursuant to an expired rental contract concluded with the municipality), the general public considered the eviction to be a political move, considering the contiguous transfer of the land to the Romanian Orthodox Church in exchange for support in the upcoming elections.[7] On behalf of the evictees, the European Roma Rights Centre sued the municipality, seeking financial compensation – unfortunately, the trial was subjected to a back-and-forth trajectory between the Cluj Tribunal and the Cluj Higher Court due to procedural

2 ECtHR 17 October 2013, No. 27013/07 (Winterstein and others v. France).

3 ECtHR 24 April 2012, No. 25446/06 (Yordanova and others v. Bulgaria).

4 ECtHR 9 October 2007, No. 7205/02 (Stankova v. Slovakia).

5 ECtHR 6 December 2011, No. 7097/10 (Gladysheva v. Russia).

6 European Roma Rights Centre, Romanian Roma Evicted to a Rubbish Dump, Hungary, ERRC, 2012, http://www.errc.org/uploads/upload_en/file/romania-report-pata-rat-17-dec-2012-en.pdf (last accessed 3 December 2023).

7 Ziua de Cluj, 'Un raport desființează primăria după ce a mutat romii de pe Coastei la Pata Rât', ZJC, 8 December 2012, https://www.zcj.ro/eveniment/un-raport-desfiinteaza-primaria-dupa-ce-a-mutat-romii-de-pe-coastei-la-pata-rat--103535.html (last accessed 3 December 2023).

issues relating to the legality of the eviction order; despite the Cluj Tribunal finding that the eviction measure had been discharged illegally, the decision was quashed, and the case was ultimately prescribed in 2017.[8] At the same time, the Desire Foundation filed a complaint with the National Council of Romania for Combating Discrimination (hereinafter: NCCD), the latter unanimously ruling that the eviction measure amounted to discriminatory treatment reflecting ethnic bias towards the Romani community and fining the Cluj Municipality with 8,000 RON (approximately 1,600 EUR).[9]

4 A Landfill as Adequate Alternative Housing?

The 'alternative accommodation' requirement developed by the ECtHR in *Yordanova and others v. Bulgaria* and subsequent case law is especially relevant in the Pata-Rât case – the 350 people forcibly evicted from their flats in Cluj-Napoca were relocated by the Romanian authorities next to the municipal landfill. Therefore, it was considered that the national authorities had discharged themselves of the obligation to aid the evictees in finding alternative housing. Such recourse does, however, give rise to the question as to what qualifies as 'alternative accommodation'. While the ECtHR does not thoroughly engage in assessing the living conditions in situations of alternative housing, it can be inferred from its reference to the ICESCR in *Yordanova and others v. Bulgaria* that the interpretation of Article 8 ECHR, and, thus, of alternative accommodation, is to be aligned with the international understanding of the right to adequate housing, as detailed by the UN Committee on Economic, Social and Cultural Rights (hereinafter: CESCR) in its General Comment No. 4.

A dwelling is to be considered adequate when, inter alia, it contains "certain facilities essential for health, security, comfort, and nutrition" such as safe drinking water, heating, energy or sanitation facilities.[10] Moreover, "housing should not be built on polluted sites" which may endanger the health of its inhabitants and should be located as such so that the dwellers have access to employment, healthcare services and education.[11] Considering these requirements developed by the CESCR, the Pata-

---

8 Muzica Instantelor, 'Romii Strămutaţi La Pata Rât Nu Mai Primesc Despăgubiri', Muzica Instantelor, https://muzicainstantelor.ro/index.php/2017/04/14/romii-stramutati-la-pata-rat-au-pierdut-procesul-cu-primaria-pentru-despagubiri/ (last accessed 3 December 2023).

9 Consiliul National Pentru Combaterea Discriminării Autoritate De Stat Autonomă, practicile discriminatorii manifestate faţă de comunităţile de romi marginalizate din oraş şi izolate în apropierea gropii de gunoi şi a staţiei de deşeuri chimice ale oraşului, 15 November 2011, http://nediscriminare.ro/uploads_ro/docManager/2990/2011_441.pdf (last accessed 28 October 2021).

10 UN Committee on Economic, Social and Cultural Rights (CESCR), General Comment No. 4: The Right to Adequate Housing (Art. 11 (1) of the Covenant), 13 December 1991, E/1992/23.

11 CESCR, 1991.

Rât ghetto can hardly be regarded adequate. According to a report submitted by Căși sociale ACUM! (an activist movement fighting for the implementation and protection of adequate housing rights for the Romani community in Romania) to the Office of the United Nations High Commissioner for Human Rights, most dwellings in Pata-Rât have no running water, sanitation facilities, heating or electricity.[12] The segregated community is at elevated risk of diseases (impaired lung function, exacerbation of chronic diseases, and poisoning with ammonia, methane, and hydrogen sulphide) due to the prolonged exposure to noxious fumes and the polluted soil and ground water from the landfill, according to the Cluj County Committee for Emergency Situations.[13] Moreover, the inhabitants live in extreme poverty, with limited access to employment or education – due to the distance between the landfill and the city and also because of the aversion of local employers towards the inhabitants of Pata-Rât. As a result, many families exclusively rely on garbage scavenging as their sole source of income. Having no legal tenure rights over their dwellings and living in informal settlements, these people are generally restricted from accessing social benefits, as they usually do not have any form of identification due to the lack of formal domicile. All these aspects effectively entrap the inhabitants of Pata-Rât in a cycle of extreme poverty and segregation, thus highlighting the symbiotic relationship between adequate housing and societal acceptance. While the inhumane housing conditions faced by the residents are the consequence of a discriminatory eviction measure (as established by the NCCD), the lack of adequate housing and resources directly impedes their reintegration into society.

5 Institutional Responses to the Crisis

The eviction measure enforced against the 350 people relocated in Pata-Rât from a block of flats in Coastei Street has been found to be fuelled by ethnic bias against the Roma community, yet little has been said about the adverse living conditions subsequently imposed on this community. The narrative constructed by the Cluj Municipality is however especially telling, considering the view expressed by the mayor – from his perspective, the relocation of Roma evictees to Pata-Rât and their subsequent segregation can only be considered beneficial to the victims.[14] Such claims reveal an intrinsic

12 Casi Sociale Acum, Humanitarian, Ecological and Housing Crisis in the Pata Rât Area of Cluj-Napoca, Romania, June 2020, https://www.ohchr.org/Documents/Issues/Housing/COVID19/CivilSociety/Casi_sociale_ACUM_Social_housing-NOW_Romania.docx (last accessed 3 December 2023).

13 Casi Sociale Acum, 2020.

14 A. Osan & V. Magradean, 'Primarul Emil Boc: S-a procedat corect cu romii de la Pata Rât; nu a fost evacuare forțată, ci cu acordul lor', Gandul, 19 February 2014, https://www.gandul.ro/stiri/primarul-emil-boc-s-a-procedat-corect-cu-romii-de-la-pata-rat-nu-a-fost-evacuare-fortata-ci-cu-acordul-lor-12114070 (last accessed 6 March 2024).

bias towards the Roma community and a distorted understanding of what 'adequate' housing represents for this ethnic minority. In the view of the mayor, the 'inadequate' living conditions of the evictees a priori to their forced evictions rendered the measure necessary – there is however only circumstantial evidence to support his claim. Against this background, it can be inferred that such justifications are construed on a prejudicial understanding of the Roma lifestyle, which is often misrepresented as foul and unkempt. It can be argued that the references made by the CESCR in its General Comment No. 4 to cultural, social, and economic factors influencing the interpretation of 'adequate housing' are misemployed by the administrative authorities of Cluj-Napoca, resulting in a discriminatory housing policy against Romani people. Throughout the decision-making process, the national authorities substituted their own prejudiced understanding of the situation for the interests of the victims, presenting the idea that the conditions in Pata-Rât are superior to those in the block of flats in which they initially resided. Such discriminatory policies further promote ethnic stereotypes against the Roma minority and entrench the segregation of this community, condemning them to a life of extreme poverty.

The systematic segregation of the Roma minority in informal settlements characterised by extremely substandard living conditions, as seen in Pata-Rât, amounts to an egregious violation of the right to adequate housing, as highlighted by the Council of Europe Commissioner for Human Rights.[15] In addition, in *Moldovan and others v. Romania*,[16] the ECtHR found that the extended exposure of the claimants to a "severely overcrowded and unsanitary environment" which negatively impacts their health and well-being, in conjunction with the dismissive attitude of the authorities, amounts to degrading treatment having the effect of diminishing the victims' human dignity. When applying this rationale to the Pata-Rât situation, the ethnically discriminatory indifference exercised by the Romanian authorities regarding the continued violations of the right to adequate housing sustained by the inhabitants of the former landfill amounts to an infringement on the human dignity of the residents.

6 Conclusion

In light of the above, the interconnectedness of the right to adequate housing and the ethnic component of the individual becomes evident – as such, socially disadvantaged minority groups are often the subject of discriminatory policies which subject them

15 Commissioner for Human Rights of the Council of Europe, Report following his visit to Romania from 31 March to 4 April 2014, Council of Europe, 2014, https://rm.coe.int/16806db83b (last accessed 3 December 2023).

16 ECtHR 12 July 2015, Nos. 41138/98 and 64320/01 (Moldovan and others v. Romania).

to substandard housing conditions, segregation and poverty. Despite harsh criticism from the international community (especially from several human rights bodies of the United Nations, such as the Human Rights Council),[17] the discriminatory attitude of the Romanian authorities regarding access to housing for its minorities remains immutable, thus highlighting the deep entrenchment of prejudice in its administrative apparatus. As such, through the policy implemented by the Cluj-Napoca Municipality, the inhabitants of the former landfill are denied the effective enjoyment of their right to housing, in its all-encompassing interpretation, due to ethnical bias. The residents of Pata-Rât are merely the exponents of the systemic failure of the authorities to protect their right to live in peace and security and, ultimately, to enjoy their human dignity. The calamitous consequences of their relocation by the landfill, as described above, highlight the position of the right to housing at the core of all economic, cultural, and social rights – the question thus remains: how can the interdependence between human rights be engaged in order to address the situation?

17 Human Rights Council, Compilation on Romania. Report of the Office of the United Nations High Commissioner for Human Rights, UN General Assembly, 9 November 2017, https://digitallibrary.un.org/record/1325016/ (last accessed 6 March 2024).

What Is a Community: Distinguishing the Right of Individuals to Housing versus the Right of Communities to Housing in the Case Law of the ECtHR

Emma Bowar

1 Introduction

A staggering size of population, about 883 million people, lives in informal settlements across the globe.[1] Often, their homes lack access to basic necessities, such as sanitation, running water, and electricity. Informal settlements and their residents are often caught between situations of economic necessity and social and legal exclusion, with few options to move elsewhere or to acquire legal ownership of the land they occupy.[2] In the case of *Ghailan and others v. Spain*,[3] the European Court of Human Rights (hereinafter: the ECtHR) was asked to consider an eviction order against an individual family residing in an informal settlement and the implications such an order had for the applicants' human rights.

2 What Happened?

The applicants alleged a violation of their right to home and private life, enshrined in Article 8 of the European Convention on Human Rights (hereinafter: the Convention), following their eviction and the demolition of their home in Cañada Real Galiana. Cañada Real Galiana is the largest informal settlement in Europe, stretching 12 km and

1 Special Rapporteur on adequate housing, Report of the Special Rapporteur on Adequate Housing as a Component of the Right to an Adequate Standard of Living, and on the Right to Non-discrimination in this Context, United Nations, 19 September 2018, https://www.ohchr.org/en/documents/thematic-reports/a73310rev1-report-special-rapporteur-adequate-housing-component-right (last accessed 6 March 2024).
2 Special Rapporteur on adequate housing, 19 September 2018.
3 ECtHR 23 March 2021, No. 36366/14 (Ghailan and others v. Spain).

housing 8,500 people, who are of mostly Roma and Moroccan descent.[4] Up until the entry into force of the Cañada Real Galiana Act in 2011, which introduced a model for the legal development of the land, Cañada Real Galiana was considered property of the public domain which could not be developed. In spite of this, informal settlements had been constructed on the land since the 1960s, and Spanish authorities were mostly tolerant of the situation. However, beginning in 2005, the Municipality of Madrid (hereinafter: the Municipality) adopted a more involved attitude with regard to Cañada Real Galiana, which led them to actively oppose new constructions. The applicants, who began building their home in Cañada Real Galiana in March 2005, were thus served with an order to suspend construction, warned of the consequences of non-compliance and received information on the administrative and judicial remedies available to them.

The applicants continued construction on their home, and they were served with a decision by the Municipality in May 2005, informing them that construction was being carried out without proper permits and that such permits could not be granted, given the designation of Cañada Real Galiana as property of the public domain. Accordingly, in June 2005, a demolition order was issued, giving the applicants fifteen days to demolish their home and informing the applicants of the available legal remedies. The applicants did not comply with this demolition order, and, in November 2006, the relevant authorities ordered the enforcement of the demolition. This was ultimately postponed, as the authorities were only able to serve the applicants this decision when they arrived to demolish the home in January 2007, and the applicants did not give the authorities their consent to enter the home. In September 2007, judicial authorisation was granted to public authorities, allowing them to enter the applicants' home to enforce the eviction and demolition against the applicants' will. Although this decision was open to appeal before the Madrid High Court of Justice, the applicants did not contest the decision, and on 18 October 2007, the applicants were evicted and their home was demolished.

On 20 October 2007, the police noted that the applicants had begun rebuilding their home in the precise location of the previous building. In November 2007, the applicants were again warned of the illegality of their actions, and in April 2008 the relevant authorities again ordered the applicants to leave their home and demolish what parts of the house had been rebuilt. This decision was not subject to appeal, as the authorities state it was merely a continuation of the previous eviction proceedings. In the following months, there was some disagreement among the authorities as to who was occupying

4 S. Jones, 'No Power, No Water, No Hope: Inside Europe's Largest Shanty Town', The Guardian, 15 January 2021, https://www.theguardian.com/world/2021/jan/15/canada-real-europe-filomena-settlement-madrid-covid-snow (last accessed 3 December 2021).

the home, but in November 2009, as well as in February 2010, the applicants were informed of the order to vacate. In November 2010, the authorities sought new judicial authorisation to enter the home to enforce the eviction and demolition against the applicants will; however, the applicants submitted observations to the ECtHR that the demolition had no legal basis. The Madrid Administrative Court ultimately granted permission to the authorities to enter the applicants' home to enforce the eviction and demolition, but postponed the order till after the school year to limit the negative effects on the children. The applicants appealed this decision and also requested review of the April 2008 decision, but these were both denied. In September 2011, the eviction and demolition were enforced, and the applicants were offered emergency housing and assistance, which they declined in favour of support from their family and social network.

The applicants lodged an appeal with the Spanish Constitutional Court, alleging violations of Article 8 of the Convention as well as Article 18 of the Spanish Constitution, which ensures the right to respect for the home. Additionally, the applicants stressed that their eviction was contrary to the purpose and spirit of the Cañada Real Galiana Act 2011, as their eviction had taken place outside the process of social dialogue. The Constitutional Court dismissed the applicant's appeal.

3 The Cañada Real Galiana Act 2011

In order to properly understand the subsequent proceedings before the ECtHR, a word must be said of the Cañada Real Galiana Act 2011, pursuant to which the property became part of the private domain. Beyond privatisation of the land, the Cañada Real Galiana Act also sought to provide municipal authorities with a framework for regularisation of the residences of Cañada Real Galiana, giving due consideration to the parties affected. It provided for the transfer of land in Cañada Real Galiana from the Autonomous Region of Madrid to the relevant municipalities, as well as to third parties within a social agreement framework. Such a framework was signed by municipalities of Madrid and Coslada in 2014, in which they agreed to address security and urban housing, with a view to ensuring the residents of Cañada Real Galiana were granted a right to housing in Cañada Real Galiana itself.

4 The Arguments of the Applicant versus the Government of Spain

In the proceedings before the ECtHR, the applicants argued that the interference with their right to a home, though in accordance with the law, had not pursued a legitimate aim or been necessary in a democratic society. In short, they believed that their eviction had been unjustified, considering the specific circumstances of Cañada Real Galiana and particularly in light of the Cañada Real Galiana Act. They believed there was no distinction between their home and the other residences of Cañada Real Galiana and as such the demolition of their individual home served no purpose. Given this, they argued that their eviction had also been disproportionate, since it had been neither necessary nor urgent, and had deeply damaged their lives and the lives of their children. Additionally, they believed that there had been insufficient safeguards with regard to the domestic proceedings and that they had not availed themselves of the available legal remedies due to the fact that the authorities had tolerated the settlements in Cañada Real Galiana for so many years.

The Government of Spain did not contest that the eviction had been an infringement of the applicant's rights under Article 8 of the Convention, but maintained that the eviction had been in accordance with the law, in pursuit of a legitimate aim and necessary in a democratic society. They stated that since the applicants had constructed their home illegally, the government had the right to recover the property. Simultaneously, the government sought to address issues such as robbery and drug trafficking prevalent in the neighbourhood. The government also argued that the eviction had been proportionate from these aims, for although the Cañada Real Galiana Act sought to regularise residences in the area, this was only meant to benefit long-term residents, not residents such as the applicants, who had only begun construction in 2005. The applicants had been informed in 2005 of the illegality of their actions and continued to be aware of this for the duration of their residency at Cañada Real Galiana. Lastly, the government argued that the applicants had not made use of the social and legal safeguards provided to them, in the form of social housing, and administrative and judicial appeal.

5 The Court's Decision: A Lawful Eviction

The ECtHR firstly re-established that the concept of 'home' found within their case law, that being that 'home' was not dependent on the legality of the dwelling, but rather on the specific circumstances of the case, wherein a continuous and sufficient link to the dwelling must be demonstrated by the applicants. As such, the dwelling in Cañada Real Galiana did qualify as the applicants' home and, therefore, derived protection from Article 8 of the Convention. The Court stated that the eviction and demolition of the applicants' home was an interference with their rights under Article 8(1) of the Convention and moved on to examine whether it was justified under Article 8(2) of the Convention.

As it was common ground between the parties, the ECtHR accepted that the interference was in accordance with the law. The ECtHR agreed with the Government that the repossession of the illegally occupied land was a legitimate aim of the authorities. The ECtHR then examined whether the interference was necessary in a democratic society, initially by reiterating that it must give a margin of appreciation to the national courts, particularly with regard to social and economic policies, who are better equipped to assess the domestic situation. However, the Court must still autonomously assess if the interference pursued a pressing social need and was proportionate to its stated aim. In considering the proportionality of the measure, the ECtHR notes that the dwelling was in fact unlawful and that the applicants had built and resided in the dwelling with full knowledge of its illegality. Additionally, although the authorities had tolerated the settlement at Cañada Real Galiana for many years, this was not true of the applicants' dwelling, and since the eviction was directed at the applicants individually, it could not be construed as targeting the community as a whole, distinguishing it from, for example, the case of *Yordanova and others v. Bulgaria.*[5] The ECtHR also noted that the applicants had at every stage of the domestic proceedings been informed of their rights to administrative and judicial review, wherein the domestic courts could have fully assessed the proportionality of their evictions as such, yet the applicants had not pursued any such review. The applicants had only contested the judicial authorisation granting public authorities with permission to enter their home without their consent, and, in this appeal, the domestic court was limited to considering the legality of the authorisation, not the eviction itself. Consequently, although exhaustive and thorough review of the demolition did not take place at the domestic level, this was due to a lack of action on behalf of the applicants and, as such, could not be held against the state. This again distinguishes it from the *Yordanova* case. The ECtHR also considered that sufficient safeguards had been provided by the authorities, particularly considering that the applicants had been offered emergency assistance which they refused, in favour of staying with their family and friends. Given the foregoing, the ECtHR considered that the eviction order had been within the margin of appreciation granted to Member States and that the subsequent actions of the domestic authorities had been proportionate to the legitimate aims pursued. As such, the ECtHR found that there was no violation of the applicant's rights to home and private life under Article 8 of the Convention.

5 ECtHR 24 April 2012, No. 25446/06 (Yordanova and others v. Bulgaria).

6 Analysing the Court's Approach to Eviction

The decision of the ECtHR in this instance follows the similar case of *Kaminskas v. Lithuania*,[6] where it found that the demolition of the applicants' illegally built home was proportionate to the aim of environmental protection sought by the government. It would appear that the ECtHR is hesitant to legitimise individual dwellings occupied illegally. This contrasts their approach to protecting informal settlements established by specific, vulnerable communities as seen in *Yordanova*. Although the applicants did argue that their eviction was part of a broader trend, as 263 demolition orders were served to Cañada Real Galiana residents between 2005 and 2010 and, in spite of the fact that 40% of Cañada Real Galiana's population is of Roma ethnicity and 26% are Moroccan nationals, they did not go so far as to contend that the eviction notices disproportionately affected a specific community.[7] As such, the ECtHR had to consider their eviction as an individual case and not an eviction of a community.

Another significant difference between the present case and the case of *Yordanova* is that – unlike the Bulgarian authorities – the Municipality of Madrid had taken steps to begin regularising many of the homes in Cañada Real Galiana, and the government of Spain did not contest the right of most Cañada Real Galiana residents to remain in their homes. The Municipality had set certain temporal limits as to who could benefit from the regularisation process, thereby excluding the applicants. However, the preference given to long-term residents by the Municipality echoes the sentiments expressed by the ECtHR itself in deciding the *Yordanova* case: due to the length of residence, a relationship to the land and a general community had been established, which created a right to stay for the residents of the community. The fact that the applicants were not long-term residents precluded them from being a part of that community.

The distinction between individual and community evictions and the time-bound definition of a community is logical given the challenges of regularising informal settlements and the importance of protecting vulnerable communities from mass evictions. However, such a black-and-white perspective seems out of place with the human connection to home and the severe consequences of eviction. Is it fair that an individual family's eviction be minimised by comparing the consequences of their eviction with the consequences of several hundred or a thousand evictions? And is it right that a concept as fluid and sociological as a community is quantified as little more than years of residence? Undoubtedly, the answer to each of these questions is not self-evident.

---

6 ECtHR 4 August 2020, No. 44817/18 (Kaminskas v. Lithuania).
7 ECtHR 23 March 2021, No. 36366/14 (Ghailan and others v. Spain).

7 Conclusion

In cases such as this, there is an obvious tension between promoting the rule of law as it is written and protecting human rights. While local law may stipulate that a specific settlement is illegal, as the ECtHR has stated, this does not completely negate the right of those residents to their home; nor does blanket illegality address the situation of necessity evident in many instances of illegal settlements. This predicament is not unique to the ECtHR, however; it is also present in planning law globally and presents a challenge to scholars and courts alike.[8]

8 S. Enemark, L. Hvingel & D. Galland, 'Land Administration, Planning and Human Rights', Planning Theory, Vol. 13, No. 4, 2014, pp. 331-348.

Previously published in Studies in Housing Law

Volume 1: Julian Sidoli, Michel Vols & Marvin Kiehl, Regulating the City: Contemporary Urban Housing Law, ISBN 978-94-6236-711-1

Volume 2: Michel Vols & Julian Vols, People and Buildings: Comparative Housing Law, ISBN 978-94-6236-802-6

Volume 3: Michel Vols & Christoph U. Schmid, Houses, Homes and the Law, ISBN 978-94-6236-974-0

Volume 4: Tom Vandromme, Nicolas Carette & Diederik Vermeir, Student Housing in Europe, ISBN 978-94-6236-267-3

Volume 5: Michelle Bruijn & Stefan van Tongeren, Navigating the Right to Housing, ISBN 978-90-4730-221-6

www.ingramcontent.com/pod-product-compliance
Lightning Source LLC
Chambersburg PA
CBHW061219240926
51846CB00006B/1278